No Place Like Home

Brooke and Marilyn,
Huntington Woods, Michigan, 1973

No Place Like Home

a memoir in 39 apartments

Brooke Berman

HARMONY BOOKS / NEW YORK

Harmony Books is a registered trademark and the Harmony Books
colophon is a trademark of Random House, Inc.

Library of Congress Cataloging-in-Publication Data
Berman, Brooke.
No place like home : a memoir / Brooke Berman. —1st ed.
p. cm.
1. Berman, Brooke.   2. Dramatists, American—20th century—
Biography.   I. Title.
PS3602.E7584Z46 2010
812'.6—dc22
[B]
2009039159

ISBN 978-0-307-58842-5

Printed in the United States of America

Design by Elizabeth Rendfleisch

1   3   5   7   9   10   8   6   4   2

First Edition

For Marilyn

Dear Reader,

I lived with a lot of people in New York City, and for the sake of clarity and to protect people I care about, most of their names (and some of their signifiers) have been changed. Some of these people (as well as a few of my friends, whose identities I'm also protecting) have been blended into composite characters. The main thing is, in each apartment I wanted to focus on where I lived, why I moved, and what I learned. I am grateful to everyone I lived with and met along the way for teaching me something vital and helping me grow.

A Manhattanite's view of the world is, basically, If it's not on this island, who cares? And while I don't share quite that much zeal around the issue, I do admit to a kind of Manhattan-centric approach to my street addresses. For the sake of clarity, all of my Manhattan addresses are listed as street address only, without borough notation. In Brooklyn or Queens, I specify the borough, and for out-of-town addresses, I specify the city.

Enjoy.

Brooke Berman
Dutch Kills, New York City
Summer 2009

contents

No Place Like Home

Getting Here
1969–1987

Huntington Woods, MI
Southfield, MI
Libertyville, IL
Northbrook, IL (twice)

I am four years old and the movers want to take the orange wool couch. I don't want them to take the orange wool couch. I don't know what they think they're doing or why all of our belongings are in brown cardboard boxes, but enough is enough. I sit on the couch in protest. I am a small four-year-old, I can't deter anyone from moving anything, but I am loud. I throw a tantrum, and, as intended, the movers stop what they're doing. My beautiful blond mother, Marilyn, comes running from the other room and lifts me off the couch so the men can get back to work. Marilyn explains that we are moving. We are going to have a new home, without my father, Harvey, who has gone to an apartment downtown. I remember nothing else about this day; later, I am told that once we arrive at the new home, a condominium in a "complex" (that's seventies for neighborhood) with twenty other identical units, I stop speaking to my mother entirely. This can't last long—she is, after all, my primary family member and the only other person living in "The Condo." So when we start speaking again, probably that night, she assures me that we will always have a home together, wherever we are.

She says, "It's you and me against the world," citing the Helen Reddy song she's begun playing incessantly since her divorce.

A word about my mom. Marilyn Lucas (Berman Kovacs Habsburg Berman) was a child prodigy who began playing her mother's piano at the age of four and debuted with the Detroit Symphony Orchestra by early adolescence. She played through college and, according to family mythology—or perhaps her own mythology, it's hard to tell the difference—turned down a chance to study at Juilliard out of fear of leaving home. She lived with her parents in Detroit until marrying my father. Marilyn used to say that she wanted to be a pianist, but she "didn't want it enough." Plus, the fear of "making it in New York" was enormous. But also, for a pretty blonde, a "nice Jewish girl" who came of age in the 1950s, the feminine mystique was way too alluring. Marilyn used to say, "I was either going to be a pianist or Doris Day."

In 1973 she is starting over. She cuts her long hair into the fashionable Mia Farrow *Rosemary's Baby* crop and goes to work as a publicist—first for the Detroit Music Hall and then in the fashion industry (or, as she calls it, "the rag business"). She takes me out with her single (mostly divorced) fashionista girlfriends, and she smokes Virginia

Slims and drinks Campari and OJ and, occasionally, borrows clothes off the rack from her jobs, returning them the next day, tags intact. It's like growing up in an extended episode of *Sex and the City*—only we're in Detroit, and the Cosmos are Shirley Temples. At least, mine are.

So when she says, "You and me against the world," it sounds okay.

We live in "The Condo" for seven years. And then Marilyn marries a bankrupt—both financially and, it turns out, morally—Austrian archduke. When she introduces him to me, she says, "His family used to rule Europe, so be nice." Helen Reddy is replaced by Barry Manilow, "Ready to Take a Chance Again," which she sings in her palomino-colored Oldsmobile Cutlass. Right away I dislike this man; I tell my mom not to trust him. Something just feels wrong about him—maybe it's the way he speaks with his foreign accent or dresses in outdated and boldly colored seventies clothes—a yellow lace shirt bought for him by his now-deceased second wife. Or maybe it's the way he coos to my mother while asking her to put dinner on her credit card instead of his. She accuses me of being "jealous" and then urges me to work on having a relationship with him. A year after their first meeting, and after the death of my father, she marries The Archduke, and we move into his house in Libertyville, Illinois—an area not particularly known for bankrupt Euro trash. Or little Jewish girls. I am ten years old. The fog is so thick the night we drive from the Detroit suburbs to Libertyville that I wonder, Does my mom know where she's going?

After two years of living in The Archduke's house, which my mother likes to the call "The Embassy" (she calls him "The Ayatollah," and she calls us "the hostages"), we move again to the North Shore suburbs, an area made famous by John Hughes in such eighties classics as *Sixteen Candles* and *The Breakfast Club*. This choice is made by Marilyn, who wants to live near other Jews, and I'm thrilled because at this point all I really want out of life is to be cast in a John Hughes movie. I even have an agent and a "stage name" (Brooke Alison—it sounds less Jewish and more appropriate for a future star of stage and screen).

Marilyn is hoping that getting out of the Libertyville house, which her husband built with his dead second wife (whom my mother has taken to calling "Rebecca" after the Daphne du Maurier thriller), will alter the tenor of her marriage. She is an optimist. First we live in an apartment complex built around a golf course, and a year later we move to a town house near a Dairy Queen. Although I get auditions—even a callback or two—no teen movies are made starring or even featuring Brooke Alison. When I'm sixteen, Marilyn and The Archduke contemplate a move to Florida, where The Archduke has started a business (and an extracurricular relationship). This plan is mercifully put to rest by my mom's health troubles—she needs to be near her family in Detroit and her doctors in Chicago. And then, when I'm eighteen years old, I leave for New York City. Forever.

So, moving wasn't anything new.

COFFEE & TEA

RAINBOW STAR

B—
I LOVE/MISS YOU, WHAT ARE YOU DOING?
B—

BROOKE BERMAN
101 THOMPSON ST.
19
NEW YORK, NY.
10012

IMMIGRATION

READING

Psychic
READER & ADVISOR

part one

"O Brave New World,
That Has Such People In't!"

New York and Providence:
1988–1993

Brooke Berman
349 Hope St.
Providence, RI
02906

brooke berman
in-progress
reading, performance
monologue
event

29 Why I Am A Hollywood Misfit

by MAR MONROE

tuesday, february 21, 8pm
dixon place
258 bowery
(between houston & prince)
ny, ny, earth...

Essential User's Guide
To the East Village

523 Cortez
Santa Fe, NM
87501

Brooke Berman
600 Bergen St.
Brooklyn, NY
11217

Barnard College Dorms, 1988–1990:
616 West 116th Street
600 West 116th Street
620 West 116th Street

An off-campus apartment:
133 West 74th Street

And a year's adventure on Hope:
349 Hope Street, Providence, RI

It is January 1988. I am eighteen years old, and I have just moved to New York City. Maybe "move" is not the right word. I'm here to go to Barnard College, but since I know that I'm never going home, there's an agenda afoot. Relocation. Like a witness protection program. I am seeking asylum from my mother and stepfather in the Midwest and their loud, frequent—and often violent—fights.

This agenda is, so far, a secret. I've left everything in my high school bedroom intact—sheets on the bed, Laura Ashley blouses in the closet—as some kind of decoy to soothe my mom so that she doesn't realize I've left her. I know in my gut I will never go back to Chicago or to her—indeed, I may never leave New York City. I've known that I wanted to live here ever since—well, really since watching reruns of Marlo Thomas in *That Girl* during my latchkey-kid years, chocolate chip cookies spread before me, television a constant—but officially since my first visit to "the City" with my mother and The Archduke for my sixteenth birthday. While all of my friends were having sweet sixteen parties, Marilyn convinced me that a trip to New York City would be a much stronger choice. To Marilyn, Manhattan was the center of all things cultural and fashionable and therefore important. I do not regret this trip. We spend a weekend at the Regency Hotel, where she used to stay with my father, ordering room service and visiting museums. Marilyn befriends the concierge, who hooks us up with theater tickets and recommendations for Italian food. One night I start talking to a chambermaid who's taking a well-earned break. She asks me how I like New York.

"I love it," I say with confidence. "I'm going to live here and be an actress."

"It's not all like this," she warns. Park Avenue hotels, taxicabs, maid service, even the view of Central Park from our beautiful suite.

I nod as if taking notes, but I have no idea what she means.

At night, after my mom and The Archduke have gone to bed, I stay up watching the lights through the window of the fancy suite. I could belong to this, I think.

Two years later I arrive at Barnard College, ready to start school, with absolutely no idea what life in the city is really like.

My first dorm room is in a college-owned apartment building on 116th Street, and it's serviceable. Okay, it's gross—a far cry from the Regency Hotel. I live in a "suite" (five rooms—three doubles and two singles) with a kitchen and a bathroom set up to look like a real Upper West Side apartment. My roommate, Margot, is a Russian Studies major from D.C. We become friends quickly and bond over the redecoration of our dorm room—most pressingly, the cold linoleum floors. We buy a large carpet scrap from the remnants section of ABC Carpet's Bargain Basement and posters from the Metropolitan Museum of Art, and we cover our door in sheet paper with a box of crayons perched on the side, like a mailbox, urging visitors to "Leave Your Art."

The dorm itself is in a neighborhood called Morningside Heights, home to Columbia University, the Manhattan School of Music, and the Jewish Theological Seminary. Today this neighborhood is gentrified, which means there are two Starbucks, a fancy grocery store, and a few Asian fusion–type eateries, but in 1988 . . . not so much. It's not rough exactly, but definitely not gentrified. There is one Italian restaurant, Caffe Pertutti (the place you take your parents); two bookstores (the good one and the less good one); an all-purpose Korean diner called The Mill (brilliant egg creams and a magazine stand) where we eat most of our meals; Amir's Falafel where we eat the rest of them; and a Chinese place, called Moon Palace, after which Paul Auster named a beautiful novel.

College is a revelation. For one thing, I've realized that much like high school, I can skip class, do the reading, and still make Bs. After being told by my freshman acting teacher that "Western culture is basically over," I decide to major not in theater but instead, following an especially charismatic professor, the interdisciplinary American Studies. After all, why show up for the bitter acting teacher when there's another, more inspired option? I spend the springtime exploring Manhattan. I take long, crazy walks, leaving my dorm on 116th Street and heading as far south as I can. I watch the neighborhoods change as I hunt for mythological coffee shops ("The Red Place" uptown, "The Green Place" downtown). And at night Margot and I sit at one of the local diners eating corn muffins with grape jelly and talking. It isn't until the middle of my sophomore year that I even see the inside of a library, and that's only because my new roommate does her homework at Columbia's Butler so that she can meet boys.

Everything about New York is magical. Everything exhilarates. But it's also overwhelmingly lonely. Plus, the money from my dad's life insurance is running out, and my stepfather has recently declared bankruptcy, so there is constant financial pressure. And I'm disappointed in the intellectual and spiritual life of college. I'd thought, based on erroneous assumptions after a summer at Bennington and a quick noncritical read of *Franny and Zooey*, that higher education would be about Enlightenment. I thought any eastern private school would be full of intellectuals, even false ones. I wanted a full-on Utopian commune where young people gathered to seek meaning. Indeed, my best friend, Grace, is having that experience at Hampshire College in western Massachusetts.

Grace is an East Coast girl I've been close to since summer camp. She represents everything about the college experience that I yearn for. Grace and her friends live together in something called "mods" and go apple picking in the orchards after reading Alice Walker essays like, en masse or something in the fields. My friends at Yale already assume they'll change the world. My friends at Brown have "dessert parties" where they feed each other sweets, argue

semiotics, and debate French poststructuralism while making plans to bus to D.C. for political marches and protests.
I don't even know what semiotics ARE. And I still think
politics means who'll win the presidential election. Here
at Columbia University, the most interesting people are
either sequestered in the library or, more likely, involved
in the social and cultural life of the city. With the exception of one week in early April, when every Columbia and
Barnard student comes out of the woodwork to play Fris-
bee and sit on the "steps" of the major campus buildings,
the student body is not accessible, not hanging around
campus.

Which I can understand. New York City is the best part.
Sophomore year, I funnel my work study funds through
the Department of Cultural Affairs and am able to get paid
for an internship at Dance Theater Workshop in Chelsea. I start to develop an off-campus life, too, and even
make an off-campus friend—Anya, a dancer who is also
the weekend receptionist at DTW. I work two or three
days a week after class, and as an intern I am often invited
to see dance and performance art events for free. I see a
lot of dance. And Anya teaches me everything about the
downtown scene. She talks to me after concerts and lectures, explaining Trisha Brown, postmodern dance (more
often called "movement"), and the aesthetics of the drag
ball. She introduces me to new ideas and new delights—
everything from panel discussions on dance and gender
to late-night exploits at the East Village performance art
bar King Tut's Wah Wah Hut. Anya helps me navigate this
strange and beautiful new world.

By now I have a crush on a long-haired Columbia philosophy student who, older than me, already knows all the

good places to eat and hang out. He lives on 110th Street, plays the guitar, frequents the Hungarian Pastry Shop, and has a girlfriend in Spain. I follow him around Morningside Heights as if he is Jesus Himself. I learn to like what he likes—falafel, the Beatles, hot chocolate made with milk instead of water, and Zora Neale Hurston. After a few months of hot chocolate and chaste backrubs, he goes to see The Girl in Spain (leaving some lame REM song on his outgoing answering-machine message). And I realize he's not my boyfriend.

It's okay, though. My real love affair is with The City, which is just like living in a Woody Allen movie with a closer view of Jersey and way more people of color than Woody's films admit. I revel in this affair, taking long walks, discovering cafés and shops, lingering in the used bookstores that (used to) litter the Upper West Side. I can spend entire weekends in film retrospectives at places like the Thalia and Bleecker Street cinemas, both of which will soon disappear. I shed the long skirts and scarves of my midwestern high school existence and buy a fringed suede jacket at the Antique Boutique, which I wear with little thrift-shop secretary-looking wool miniskirts and combat boots.

But here's the thing—after a year and a half of college, I decide it's not for me. I file for a leave of absence, telling my mom that maybe I'll go back someday, then take the final installments of my late father's life insurance and move to Providence, Rhode Island, to study with Anne Bogart, the experimental theater director who has recently taken over the Trinity Rep Company and Conservatory. It's a fine plan. Trinity Rep is an award-winning regional theater with

a school attached, and I can go there, focus on my "training," and still hang out with people my own age at Brown—
the semiotics crew and their dessert parties! I've known for
a while that I want to be an actress and do the very specific
kind of work that Anne specializes in. I imagine becoming
some new combination of Spalding Gray, Meredith Monk,
and Sandra Bernhard. Anne's work uses a physical and
gestural vocabulary, along with visual imagery and composition principles, to teach actors to be full "creators," to
move beyond the psychological interpretation of text. Anne
likes multidisciplinary, intelligent "performers" who can
bring their whole selves to the overall process of inventing a
play. This is a far cry from the teachers I've had so far, who
say things like "you're too smart to be an actress."

....

133 West 74th Street
349 Hope Street, Providence, RI

So in August 1989, after two months in an apartment off
campus, wherein the actual floor space is big enough only
for the unrolled futon, and the lack of AC drives me to
take up my great-grandma Celia's habit of putting a bowl
of ice cubes in front of a fan, I move to Providence. I live
in a pale blue Victorian house built in the 1850s (on the
aptly named Hope Street), with a dance studio in the attic.
My room is *enormous*, with a king-size futon on a raised
platform—I need a step stool to get into bed every night—
and windows on three sides, which mean the most gorgeous
sunsets ever. It is one of the best years of my life, one in

which I am fully dedicated to training. My classmates and I are at the theater six days a week, from 9 A.M. to 6 P.M. (at the earliest), taking classes in acting, directing, "composition," tai chi, aikido, ballet, and "performance aesthetics." When we're not in class, we're working on the "The Mainstage," performing small roles in the professional company's theatrical season. I appear in two of the company's productions that year—first as a "Gray Person" (basically background noise) in Anne's production of a Gorky play, and then as a sex-crazed teenage orphan who fakes a virgin birth in an adaptation of the Chilean novel *The Obscene Bird of Night*. And I perform my first-person solo theater monologues at postshow cabarets.

I'd been so miserable and lonely in school that I'd started to think the problem must be me. And that it (me) would never get better. At Trinity Rep, engaged in a professional training program with a peer group of (mostly older) fellow actors and dancers and directors (and the occasional crush from Brown University), I know that the only thing wrong was I was in the wrong place! Anne's classes fill every need, attend to every hunger. She asks us to consider what makes a play. Creating theater, she says, is about creating memory. What makes a memory? What ancient ritual (or new set of codes) are we enacting when we walk into a theater and sit down, with strangers, to share two hours in what my friend Joanna will later call "a small dark holy space"? And how are we changed by the experience? My mind expands. My body releases (all that ballet and tai chi!), and my heart lightens. When the year ends and Anne leaves Trinity Rep, I leave too. Excited to start a working life in earnest, I move back to New York City.

Regretfully, I tell my college adviser and my mother that I'm not going back to school but instead am starting a professional theater career. Both of them take it remarkably well. My adviser gives me her blessing; my mom gives me her American Express card.

I'm twenty-one years old. I'm ready.

....

340 East 9th Street

In October 1990 I rent a room in an apartment on East Twelfth Street, sight unseen, from an ad in the classified section of the *Village Voice*: Room for rent. One bedroom in a downtown 2BR on tree-lined block. I am shocked when I arrive to find out (1) how small my room is and (2) how much more I'll be paying than the leaseholder, Paul, a long-haired but balding musician whose room is twice the size of mine. He's making money off me!? I've never heard of such a thing. I've incorrectly assumed that we're splitting the rent, or that I would be paying less because my room is so much smaller. And I don't discover the truth from Paul directly, but from an overheard phone call the day I move in.

Furious, I confront him. Paul tells me that this is how things are done in New York real estate and that I am lucky to have a room in this neighborhood, the East Village, which will soon be too expensive for any of us. I tell him to fuck off, and I haul my five unopened boxes back to the rental car, which I will have to return, driving tearfully to a friend's dorm room at Barnard. *Now what?*

I can't ask my mother for help. Marilyn is still processing the information that I won't be going back to school (I
tell her, *there's no more money for school, maybe later, someday . . .*) and
even worse, that I won't be living in a doorman building.
She has no idea what it costs to rent an apartment in any
building, let alone those with doormen, or why her friends'
kids can afford to live in them while I cannot. (Her friends'
kids either work in finance or are being supported by their
parents. Easy answer to an easy question.) Nor does she
take into account that I don't care about things like doormen; I'm in New York to feed my artistic pursuits. I'm
doing the one thing my mother always told me I could do—
pursue my dreams—and yet every action I take is foreign to
her. And thus, terrifying.

But also, practical advice has never been my mother's
thing. Life with Marilyn is more like a big party where
things get broken and you consume too much of everything
and feel bad later, but there are at least one and probably two really stunning moments of intimacy and a good
lucid middle-of-the-night conversation and a surprise
dance in high-heeled shoes. She brings warmth and music.
Practical advice ranges from how to find a good nail salon
("Make sure they sterilize their equipment and trim your
cuticles!") to how to fit a bra (a real lifesaver). The most
useful thing she has ever taught me was how to pack for a
weekend away: *"Only take carry-on. And roll your clothes instead of
folding them. You save room and prevent wrinkling."* To be fair, as an
adult, I am incredibly grateful for my mother's insights and
advice. But finding an apartment or a job, saving money,
or even balancing a checkbook is just not her domain. And
although she wants more than anything to be able to tell

me what to do, we both know (even if I'm the only one
who'll admit it) that she's out of her league. Which means
these conversations often end in tears or screaming. Or
both. She tells me to use her credit cards, then confides
that she's "el broke-o." She berates me for not knowing
someone who can help me, then berates herself for not
marrying a man who could afford to pay my way. I tell her
that I don't care about those things, and I don't want The
Archduke anywhere near me, let alone paying my bills. I'm
still angry about the odious way he treats my mother. But
that's no longer my problem.

I realize that if I am to survive in New York, I will have
to learn everything Marilyn couldn't teach me—I will have
to figure out how, without a college degree, I can earn
enough money to stay here.

I make a list of everyone I know who might connect me
to gainful employment and, one by one, call or visit each,
telling them that I'm looking for work. I am optimistic and,
without too much trouble, get a two-week temp job covering for the receptionist at PS122, an experimental dance/
theater/performance center in the East Village.

I also have a therapist, a woman I started seeing through
Barnard health services the summer I left school. She
points out that the longer I spend trying to get "settled,"
the more obstacles I face in beginning to establish a career.
She says, "Without an apartment, you're deliberately keeping yourself in limbo." And I nod. But I don't know how
to do it any better, or really what else to do. I'm not in the
position to, say, go to a real estate agent, give him or her
my dad's business card, claim someone as a guarantor, and
take an apartment. I am left to the mercy of the *Village Voice*

classified section, the "roommate wanted" ads, and thrown to the kindness of strangers,

I do want to get settled. And I do want to "move on" with "my career." I have big plans. I've come back to New York from Providence with the goal of working as a solo performance artist, as the base for a more substantial acting career. A lot of people are doing this kind of work—Spalding Gray is my idol, John Leguizamo my crush. And meanwhile, answering phones at PS122, I'm meeting everybody and learning. Deb Margolin says, "Virtuosity isn't as important as hunger. Follow your deepest hunger." And Ann Carlson says, "Make the work that delights you, the work you want to see."

My first week at my substitute receptionist post, I tell someone the story of the unethical and badly coiffed Paul, and to my great surprise she offers me a house-sitting gig. So now I have a place to go!

Janie is a beautiful theater and installation artist (She makes puppets! And films! And she draws!) on her way to San Francisco for a two-week residency at the art space Life on the Water. Janie offers me her apartment, a floor-through on East Ninth, saying that I'm doing her a favor by getting her mail and looking after her things. I can't believe my good fortune.

The night before the downtown house-sit, I take myself to hear music at the coffeehouse in the crypt of St. Paul's Chapel, a key part of my former life as a Barnard undergrad, and stay up until sunrise talking to a Mormon I meet over cider at the "bar." He and I leave St. Paul's for Tom's, the diner on 112th Street, and then leave Tom's for the boy's apartment.

"I'm a virgin," I say. "I won't have sex with you."

"I'm a Mormon," he says. "I won't have sex with you, either."

So it's perfect. Once at his place, we make out (he doesn't remove the special underwear, but I do get to see it), and he offers to help me move. I think he must be joking. I go back to the dorm room at 5 A.M., as the sun is rising, and four hours later I'm shocked by his phone call. He asks, "What time are we moving?"

This sweet stranger carries my five boxes up the stairs to Janie's. When he sees the place, he says, "You're a lucky girl." I am a lucky girl indeed. Everything about being here, this apartment and proximity to Janie, inspires me. She is the kind of adult I want to become—a full-time, self-supporting artist with a floor-through apartment in the East Village. I take note of each detail, big and small. Big: Everything is painted white—white floors, white walls, white ceilings, white doors—except for her brightly colored folk-art paintings and puppet displays. Small: Janie keeps her espresso in a glass jar (and now I will, too) in the mini-fridge in her little artist's kitchen (*Note:* Artists don't need full-size refrigerators). It all amazes me. The first week is heaven. And then I start to worry. I have to find another place to live. After all, Janie is only gone for two weeks, and each day carries me closer to her return and my move-out date.

But I'm in luck! Just in time, a friend from Providence calls. He wants me to meet his best friend who has a room for rent in her two-bedroom apartment just two blocks away from where I'm staying now. The girl is asking $550 for the second bedroom. The apartment itself is a six-floor walk-up with no bathtub, and the room is barely large enough to fit a futon. But it's close and cheap and the rent is split evenly, and

I have just enough money. She's not even asking for a deposit.
I call her up and ask, "When can I move in?"

....

117 East 7th Street

Jen is a wealthy Southerner attending NYU's Tisch School
of the Arts. She has been living in this East Village walk-up
for about a year. At first there was a roommate. Then there
wasn't. She has family money, so she's not really concerned
about it, but she wants to be "responsible." Which means
she wants to split things down the middle. She is also
recovering in Overeaters Anonymous, so I'm not allowed
to bring refined sugar into the house. At this point, my
eating habits are ridiculous—like Grape-Nuts and skim
milk. For every meal. And as Grace points out while we're
talking on the corner pay phone as I'm trying to finish an
entire pint of Ben & Jerry's because I can't take the car-
ton home with me, Jen's compulsive behavior incites me to
compulsions of my own. But, truthfully, I could use a little
discipline when it comes to sugar. I still think it's permissible to call ice cream "dinner."

As for the apartment itself, the word "small" takes on
new meaning. The entire apartment is roughly five rooms:
entryway/hallway/kitchen, her room, my room, a sort
of living room with a futon couch, and a tiny bathroom
just big enough for a stall shower and a toilet. Jen has
installed a countertop in the "kitchen," which is really a
big hallway with a stove and a refrigerator. In her bedroom
she's installed the loft bed that is common to East Village

apartments around this time. Jen sleeps in the loft and "lives"—mostly meditates—beneath it. There isn't room for much else.

My room does not have a loft bed, but Jen has an extra futon, which she lets me use. The futon takes up the entire surface area of the tiny room's floor. During the day I roll it up and push it against the wall. I create a makeshift desk out of two milk crates with a (found) purple board on top. I sit on the floor, cross-legged, to write. The best thing about my room is the ample closet. I am too inexperienced in NYC real estate to realize how rare it is to have a real closet. At this point, the only belongings I have are books and clothes—so the closet is important. I store my books on the shelf in the closet and hang all of my clothes. I find a third milk crate on the block and bring it upstairs to house dresser-type items—socks, underwear, T-shirts. I buy a basket for sweaters on Eighth Street, placing it above the milk-crate dresser, and all is well with the world.

Now for a job. My first temp job, at PS122, has ended. I have signed up to be the "alternate receptionist" (meaning, if you get sick call me, and I'll take your shift) there and at DTW, but there's no guarantee that anyone will call. It's time for gainful employment, something stable. And I realize I have no skills. None. I've spent my childhood with upwardly mobile debtors and my young adulthood at an Ivy League college taking classes like "African American Literature and the Vernacular" and in an experimental theater program learning something called "the Six Viewpoints," which is a way of creating and talking about postmodern performance. So I can deconstruct multicultural literature, improvise physical theater scenarios, and write monologues. And I can answer phones and do dishes (barely), but I've never had to pay my own way before, and as a twenty-one-year-old without a college degree or training in anything besides theater and dance, I have no idea what I will do.

When I left home at eighteen for college, my mother gave me two now-infamous pieces of advice: "One," she said, "always separate your laundry into light and dark loads; otherwise, it all turns gray. And two, please don't swallow semen. There is an AIDS crisis." And then, she handed me her Saks Fifth Avenue credit card "for emergencies." And although I still forget to separate my clothes and I have yet to be faced (no pun intended) with an actual penis, I do know what to do at Saks. In fact, when I run out of optimism and have worked myself into an anxious mess from too many classified ads and letters to potential employers, I take the 6 train uptown and wander around the legendary department store. I know too much about my mother's finances to actually buy anything—it's more of a museum experience. I meander through the store, looking at colors, textures, shapes—sometimes I touch things— with that card in my pocket and thus the knowledge that if I really, really want to make a purchase, I can. There is power in this. I think it's behind most of my mother's life as a consumer. With this plastic card, nobody will turn me away. And looking is—honestly—enough to restore my faith in the human condition. Like Holly Golightly says about Tiffany's, nothing very bad can happen here. Plus, if I can't get actual mothering from the actual Marilyn, the least I can do is go to Saks.

I get a job waiting tables at a short-lived breakfast joint

on Second Avenue. But one day I leave for a rehearsal without having covered my shift and come back to find I've been replaced. The avant-garde dance/theater piece that I'm rehearsing pays something like $50 a week, so I need another job right away.

I go back to looking. I want to say yes to everything. And indeed I try everything. I visit a temp agency but balk when they tell me I have to wear panty hose and learn to type. I cater but get upset after being recognized by an acquaintance from my theater pursuits who is a guest at the party I'm working—even worse, I have to stay and clean up. I start ushering for concerts and lectures at the Metropolitan Museum of Art. (I particularly like the ones running in conjunction with the current exhibit, "The Russian Imagination." I leave a lecture thinking, Oh! I'm not crazy! I'm just a Russian-Polish Jew!) I have to work a lot of ushering shifts in order to pull in any decent money, but it's worth it to be in the museum soaking up culture. I pretend it's an adult-ed program. My mother is pleased, but even more so when I go on a date—my first in New York City, possibly my first ever. The date is with a twenty-eight-year-old Finance Guy who works in the newly formed Tribeca Film Center and lives in a loft. He takes me to see *Cyrano* starring Gérard Depardieu and out for pizza, and I'm kind of shocked to discover I actually like him. We plan a second date. Things are starting to fall into place.

And then, one day in January 1991, just after the Gulf War breaks out (and I attend my first antiwar protest), Jen comes home with an announcement. "I'm rich," she says as if she's never given it much thought before. "I don't have to live like a starving artist. And after class today, after having this epiphany, I walked right out of NYU and into a broker's

office where I leased a 1BR in a high-rise. It has phenom-
enal views, and I move in February 15. Want this place?"

I'm shocked. Not only because I *do* have to live like a
"starving artist" but also because I thought it was going so
well. "I think we're becoming real friends," I had said to
her not more than a month ago. (She replied, "I don't
think we're becoming friends," letting me know that real
friendship takes a while. But soon we really would become
friends.) Immediately I decide that I don't want to try to
hold on to 117 East 7th Street. I'm twenty-one years old,
and it doesn't even occur to me that a lease on a 2BR in the
East Village for $1,195 would be a good thing. I just think,
tiny bedrooms, no bathtub, the walk up those five flights
every day, sometimes more than once? No, no, I don't
want this apartment or the responsibility of finding the next
roommate. No.

So with roughly three weeks' advance notice, I start
looking for a new place to live. It is the first time that I will
go through rituals that will become second nature later. I
spend every Wednesday morning with the *Village Voice* spread
across the floor, calling ads from the classifieds. I'm looking for a "share" and have circled all the ads that fall within
both my price range and neighborhood requirements
("What's Murray Hill?"), but when it comes to calling, I
freeze. What do I say? What makes a good roommate?

I go with the basics: "My name is Brooke. I'm looking
for a room to rent in a share. I can pay up to five hundred dollars." I look at every single apartment I can. A Park
Slope 4BR inhabited by Wiccan undergrads. (I don't mind
that they're Wiccan; I do mind that they've painted every
room day-glo green.) A Lower East Side loft owned by an
older woman artist, someone with black and white pictures

of herself showing her work at the Whitney Biennial. (Or was she sleeping with someone who was showing? I can't remember. But I do remember, she was gorgeous.) This woman fascinates me, and I stay longer than I should, listening to her stories. She is a geriatric version of the girls who presently intimidate me. Now, with failing health and finances, she needs a roommate. What happened, I wonder, between the tough art-chick with the shag haircut in those pictures and this moment? Why is she alone? I am tempted to take the room, but I have enough Mama Drama of my own without adding a surrogate.

More apartments. A Chelsea 1BR converted to two, common fare in New York City: Someone who can't afford their nice apartment decides to live in the "living room" and rent out the "bedroom," usually for more than half the rent since they are, after all, living in the living room. But I'm willing to do it—the neighborhood is amazing. The lovely, long-haired woman renting the room refuses my application, saying, "You're adorable, but you're a baby." A duplex share with five other girls on lower Broadway, just below Church Street, is premium real estate, but nobody's room costs more than $600. I must not be fabulous enough for the five TriBeCa girls; they don't call me in for a second interview. (Callbacks? For an apartment? Really?) To Brooklyn, where a choreographer's sister needs a flatmate—her current roommate, a gay rights activist, is moving in with his boyfriend. Their place is a floor-through on Smith Street in the then-empty Boerum Hill. I have never had a particularly good sense of the "up and coming," and to me this neighborhood seems desolate. In a few years' time, of course, I'll be proven wrong. But again, I am barely twenty-two and naive about New York real estate. A woman at a secondhand store on First Avenue tells me that "everyone's moving to Williamsburg. Seriously, it's like the next East Village." And I think, Really!?

What I don't yet know is what every prospective roommate wants to hear: "I'm employed, I'm responsible, I work during the day, so you'll never see me. And I'm clean." Instead I say things like, I'm an actress and aspiring performance artist. I went to Barnard. I don't drink or smoke, but I do have an active social life. I see a lot of dance. I have a lot of different jobs, and none of them are particularly stable. I don't know how I'm supporting myself, but I'm determined to not be my mother, so I take whatever job comes my way. No wonder *nobody* wants me to move in.

I go to the Finance Guy's loft after apartment hunting. He takes me out and introduces me to both sushi and TriBeCa, both of which become enduring loves, even as he does not. (He teaches me to use chopsticks on the same night he shows me what a hand job is. The two are forever linked in my mind.) Finance Guy has definite opinions about the way I'm living my life. He says I'm making it "harder than it needs to be." He says, "I don't get it. You're smart, verbal, and talented. Why not get a real job?"

What he doesn't do is tell me what a real job is or how to apply for one. He doesn't introduce me to anyone who could help me. He just pays for dinner, and then resents me when I can't contribute. But it's not his fault. Chelsea Lady was right—I am a baby. I know *nothing* about men and women—I'm still a virgin for God's sake, which means we are not having real official intercourse sex. Also, I'm not in love with him. I'm dating him because I feel like I should. And I do like him. He is an amateur photographer, and I like when he shoots pictures and shows them to me. I like when we go to see movies at the intelligentsia haunt Film Forum, and I really like how he makes coffee in the morning (in a French press, a habit I will later adopt) when I spend the night. I try to explain to him that I want to be an actress and a performance artist. A "real job" would distract me from my purpose. Years later, when I am twenty-seven, I too will hear this same excuse from my own twenty-two-year-old boyfriend. I guess it's a rite of passage.

By Valentine's Day Jen has sublet our East Village apartment to a Canadian rock band named after a Hitchcock film, and I have made no progress on the room-for-rent front. In fact, I have nowhere to go. Maybe I'm hoping Finance Guy will invite me to stay with him, but he does not. (Why would he? We're not even having sex!) And so, without any other options, I move to the high-rise with Jen and pay rent to sleep on her sofa bed. She says she would feel resentful if she let me stay there for free, but if I paid her, even though she doesn't technically need the money, she would feel that the whole thing was fair. I really just don't know any better, and my therapist is trying to break me of the (inherited) notion that anyone owes me anything or that it's anybody else's responsibility to take care of me. So I pay Jen $350 to sleep on her foldout couch for a month. This makes *me* resent *her*. But no one is thinking much about that in March 1991.

I discover the following: I hate high-rises. I hate doormen. I hate the East Twenties, a neighborhood primarily defined by *not* being the East Village and also *not* being the tonier, more exclusive Gramercy Park (where they will shoot the film version of Edith Wharton's *The Age of Innocence*).

I very much want to hate Jen, but in fact I don't hate her. I can't even hold resentment longer than a day or two. She's kind of weirdly great. And once Finance Guy and I break up—he has another girlfriend, someone his own age, and he quickly dumps virginal me for someone who'll actually put out—it is comforting to come home to her. We meditate together and eat brown rice. She forces me to reconsider my entire relationship to sugar. I copy her CDs and thus share in her love of Prince. I discover the unmitigated joy of walking up Fifth Avenue with a Walkman playing "Under the Cherry Moon." By the time I move out, she feels like family. (Note the use of the F Word. It will come back later.) But Jen is not family. And in some way I don't yet want to admit to understanding, paying Jen for that month is the right thing to do. Even though it theoretically sucks to have to pay someone money to live on a pullout sofa bed, the fact of the matter is we're not related, and she doesn't owe me anything. This will become relevant again, ten years later, when I am living with Emma. But we're not there yet. And some lessons take a long time to learn.

600 Bergen Street, Brooklyn

By April 1, 1991, I am off Jen's sofa bed and have moved to Prospect Heights, Brooklyn, to live in a house with Anya, my friend from Dance Theater Workshop. A real house! A duplex! I hire a "Man with Van" whose number has been posted on the bulletin board at the Screen Actors Guild (one of the places where I have been stalking rooms to rent). The Man with Van is in his fifties, and he looks like someone's dad except that he's wearing a beret. We have only those original five boxes to carry, plus the purple board and two milk crates that make up my "desk," and the third milk crate, aka "the dresser." During the drive, when I mention that I'm an aspiring actress and that I've begun writing my own performance material, he gives me advice on dialogue. At this point, I have no idea that I will become a playwright, and I think his advice is a strange gift, but I take it nonetheless. He tells me to listen in to conversations and write them down—every day. He says, "Go to public places, take a notebook, and write down what people say verbatim." This is advice that I not only follow but also still give to my own students when I teach. There is no other way to learn the (often illogical) musicality of speech than to copy the music. Write down what people say. This advice is quite a gift for an hour and a half's move to Brooklyn. By the time we hit Flatbush Avenue, I have ammunition for a career that I don't yet know is in my future.

The house on Bergen is spacious—a relief after East Village walk-ups. My room is upstairs, next to the kitchen and bathroom, while the other bedrooms (and thus room-mates) are on the main floor. The room is furnished with a twin bed and a dresser. It has an enormous closet. I am subletting from a *Village Voice* writer who will, years later, disappear on Mount Rainier in a surreal accident—he goes bird-watching and *never comes back*! But in 1991 the writer is on a fellowship in Mississippi. He has left Anya, who lives in the big room downstairs, in charge of finding the right subletter, and Anya insists that person is me. In fact, she has been "insisting" ever since Jen gave up Seventh Street—but it is only now that I am open or desperate enough to listen.

Anya is both role model and art-crush with her "Every-thing I Need to Know I Learned in Art Class" approach to the world. She can do anything with a glue gun and some glitter: clothes, decorating, cooking even. Most of her friends live in the neighborhood, so weekends in Brook-lyn (and evenings for that matter) are always full of activ-ity. Plus, Anya has been initiating me into the subculture of Lower East Side dance and performance art since I was in college. She takes me to Veselka, a Ukrainian diner on Ninth Street where the artists hang out eating the most amazing poppy-seed cake ever, and to symposiums and workshops at Movement Research, a dance organization, and to parties full of the most interesting new people—and now she initiates me into Brooklyn.

Anya has also hooked me up with a job as wardrobe assis-tant for a dance company that she's begun working with—so she truly has my back. As wardrobe assistant, I pack the company to go on tour, making sure each costume is cor-rectly labeled and cataloged, and when the company returns to New York, I do their laundry. It's a great job because (1) I love clothes, especially dance costumes, which remind me of being six and playing dress-up at my grandma's house, and (2) when I do their laundry, I throw in my own.

My mother is horrified to hear that I've moved to Brooklyn. It makes her think of gangsters and old Rus-sian Jews on the boardwalk—*A Tree Grows in Brooklyn,* Coney Island, *Radio Days.* She insists that this is retrograde motion, not understanding how gentrified parts of Brooklyn have become, or how many young people are claiming these neighborhoods. If she only knew. If I only kept the lease. If only there were a lease.

That spring (in the Slope or the Heights, depending on

what side of Flatbush one stands) is all about nesting. I buy
a green nylon jacket at the Salvation Army and wear it every
day with a Brooklyn baseball cap turned backwards and
high-top sneakers. I cut my long hair. I finally look like an
artist. I develop neighborhood rituals like coffee with milk
and sugar from the little truck outside the police station on
Bergen Street on my way into the city for work. And pizza
from the Italian guys on the corner. I devote one full day
a week to Brooklyn—and on that day I only travel to places
I can walk, like across Flatbush and into Park Slope. The
Slope itself is still full of hippies and dancers. No baby car-
riages yet. No Starbucks. Instead, small, local businesses.
Occasionally a Blue Man from the Blue Man Group. And
Anya makes sure that on the weekends we hit her favorite
diner, the Silver Spoon. But by the time I settle down and
find my Brooklyn rhythms, it's time to start looking for the
next place to go. By the end of June, the *Village Voice* writer
will return home and want his room back. Wishing I could
stay, wishing Anya were "family," I start the search again.
This time, however, I'm prepared. I am more organized.
I understand how it works. I have some money saved from
my assortment of spring jobs, which have changed only
slightly in that I've stopped ushering and taken over Anya's
old job as weekend receptionist at Dance Theater Workshop. I have also been trained at DTW to bundle and sort
mail. This is the job that will stay with me—and eventually
provide health insurance—for the next five years.

As an arts service organization, DTW maintains a
not-for-profit status with the post office that allows its
member-artists to send their concert announcements out
at the unbelievably low third-class "bulk" rate. Thus, DTW
also maintains a staff member (or two) who can bundle and

sort third-class mail according to post office regulations and then file paperwork for the mailing. I train to do this job as an alternate so that the large German dancer who currently does the job can go on vacation. Within a few months, I will take over the job entirely and become "services assistant" in charge of all third-class mailings. I make $12 for every thousand pieces of mail that I bundle and sort and sticker and schlep to the Old Chelsea Post Office. There, the bags of mail fall into the care of the gentlemanly John Cheetwood, a man who not only processes all of Chelsea's third-class mail but does so with a kind word and a smile.

The point is, I now know something about looking for an apartment and holding a job. When I start to look again, in May 1991, I have a little money and a little more experience. Plus, I have a roommate!

Margot, my freshman college roommate from Barnard, the girl with the Cyrillic alphabet on the wall, wants to find a place together. She's about to graduate (along with the other members of my freshman class) and wants to live in lower Manhattan—with me. We start meeting on Wednesday mornings to comb the *Voice* ads together and make calls from her dorm room, and without too much trouble, after a few weeks of looking, we discover the first place that I will think of as "home."

....

101 Thompson Street

We stumble into 101 Thompson, a "converted 2BR" legal sublet in a beautiful co-op building—on a prime block—

because, while checking out a ridiculously small 1BR in the neighborhood, the real estate broker runs into a friend who says, "Do you guys want to look at my place? I kind of think I should move." It seems impulsive (for her, if not us) but we agree, and two weeks later we're signing a lease with Marc, a hottie Wall Street type who owns this place but rents it out to pay for his mortgage in Brooklyn. Marc the Landlord seems to enjoy the cute twenty-two-year-olds moving into his apartment—especially when, in the absence of stamps, I hike down to Wall Street to deliver the rent in person. My first week in the apartment, an old friend says, "You belong here. This is your neighborhood." And I believe him.

The former tenant has left her double bed in the bedroom that will be mine with a note, assuming that I'd want to keep it. It takes me a while to realize that, in fact, I do. At first I complain, "Why won't that girl come get her bed?" and then I remember one of my grandmother Ida's favorite sayings: *When life gives you lemons, make lemonade.* Life has given me a bed, so I keep it and, with the money I am saving, purchase nice sheets from Macy's and a second-hand dresser from Furniture Bob, a gruff but bighearted man who has set up shop in the empty lot across from Time Café. Furniture Bob strips the dresser for me and offers free delivery. He says, "I just want to make the furniture move." Over the next few weeks, I'll stop to chat at Furniture Bob's on a regular basis. He has a dedicated band of hot twenty-something girls stripping furniture (and God knows what else) for him—and he's quite a conversationalist.

The adopted bed takes up most of the space in my room. The dresser and my now-standard board-and-milk-crate desk take up the rest. There is no closet. Instead, some previous tenant has installed a heavy pole from one corner to another, and I hang my clothes from that. French doors open the entire space onto the one "commons room"—a makeshift living room/kitchen/foyer area. Our bathroom is tiny—even tinier than Jen's in the East Village—so small that the sink and mirror are both located outside of the room itself, in the "foyer"—i.e., directly opposite the door to the apartment. The one flaw to the entire apartment is that we have no bathtub, a minor catastrophe as far as I'm concerned. I befriend a Canadian girl who waitresses nearby and every now and then, I pick up her keys and walk across town, where I take long, luxurious baths in her rent-controlled studio. She even lets me use her Queen Helene face products. It is an incredibly sweet gesture, one I am grateful for. After all, what's a Piscean without her bathtub?

Margot and I are paying for location—prime SoHo, Prince and Thompson. And our apartment is cheap by neighborhood standards. We pay a total rent of $1,100—unheard of today. I pay less than Margot—$500 to her $600—because she has the bigger room with the actual door.

Once unpacked, I start to explore all of the won-ders and delights of SoHo. In 1991, this feels like a "real" neighborhood—full of the appropriately sweet mix of Italian grandmothers and young artists and writers. I meet all of my neighbors. Across the hall, Mary (with her dog, Candy) has lived in this apartment building for her entire adult life. Mary, with her housedresses and raspy ex-smoker's voice, moved to Thompson (from nearby Sullivan) when

she married her husband. His family had an apartment
in the building and a bar down the street. He and Mary
opened a candy store, hence the dog's name. Mary likes to
leave her door open during the summer, for ventilation,
so I get a good look inside—a lot of pink. I feel honored
when she starts inviting me over for coffee, even asking me
to help her with her eyedrops (I gladly oblige). She fills me
in on the history of the neighborhood, what it was like when
Italian social clubs lined the streets, before the eighties artists (and then nineties boutiques) started moving in. Next
door to Mary, another actor, Dino, lives in a "family apartment." And downstairs, a sweet Australian composer, his
wife, and their baby daughter live and work and play music.
The super is a newlywed actor from Minnesota with a gorgeous wife and infant, and he turns out to be an old friend
of new friends of mine. 101 Thompson is a regular family.

SoHo lives up to every fantasy I've ever had about life as
an artist in New York. It's not as scary as Avenue C, where
three dancer friends have moved into a loft across from a
vacant lot. And not as far as Brooklyn, where I lived with
Anya. I can walk to all of my jobs and, best yet, walk home
alone at night, no matter what time of day, safe along the
well-lit streets. I take pleasure in discovering every quirk of
my neighborhood, every insider gem—from $1.85 break-
fast specials (Bella's and Buffa's) to gnarly coffee shops
(Auggie's—best beans, surliest postpunk staff). I find out
where Laurie Anderson eats breakfast (Moondance) and
start going there regularly. I make friends at the local café,
the local bookstore, the Laundromat, even the butcher—
and I'm about to become a vegetarian! Bernard the French
Butcher loves to flirt and is outraged when I tell him I'm

still a virgin, adamant that I can turn that mess around if only I learn to hide my intelligence.

I will live in this apartment for the next two and a half years. I will feel stable, grounded, and happy. And as promised by the Upper West Side therapist, the experience of a solid home will indeed contribute to my ability to create a base in the world—to write and produce and perform, to invest in community, make friends, and spread out.

In the fall of 1991, The Archduke has a massive stroke and despite their profound and now impossible-to-ignore marital troubles, my mother devotes herself to his care. They have moved back to Detroit so that Marilyn can take a corporate job with the health benefits she so desperately needs. And The Archduke has just begun to create work for himself, as a consultant, when the stroke hits, causing aphasia and paralyzing an entire side of his body. I fly to Detroit to be by my mother's side in the ICU. I don't yet know how intimate I will become with the intensive care unit at Beaumont Hospital. Neither does she.

It is worth mentioning here that my mother was a diabetic who developed severe kidney disease while I was in high school. During my junior year, she and The Archduke traveled to the Mayo Clinic in Minnesota, where she was put on a strict low-protein diet, ostensibly to correct and address the kidney failure. Six months later she came to terms with the fact that, whether she liked it or not, she'd need a transplant. She spent the fall of 1986 on dialysis (I often missed school or arrived late to drive Marilyn to the dialysis unit or pick her up, helping her to get home in one piece when The Archduke was unavailable, which was often). In November of 1986, after roughly six weeks of dialysis, Marilyn had her first transplant. "A new me," she said with pride. But the antirejection medication which she now takes daily is expensive, and she has not had proper coverage since The Archduke's bankruptcy. Her new corporate job solves a number of problems, not the least of which is health insurance, for both her and her husband. But she was not expecting this.

When I arrive, she is holding steady, full of New Age platitudes and affirmations, determined to will her husband into a full recovery.

My mother has the gift of positive thinking. Nobody is allowed to say anything remotely pessimistic in the actual hospital room. She forces the doctors to go into the hallway if they want to say anything that isn't 100 percent full of sunshine. And then, after listening to them, she goes back inside the room to pronounce to her conscious but ailing husband, at the top of her lungs in case his hearing is gone too, "YOU ARE GOING TO BE JUST FINE . . . YOU ARE JUST FINE."

I fly back to New York relieved and also frightened. It's no longer Brooke and Marilyn against the world. But in the cab on the way home from the airport I think, who wants to be *against* the world at all? I vow that from here on out, it's Brooke *With* the World. This relationship will be cooperative, collaborative, and co-creative. A solo stint, post-Marilyn, like Diana Ross without the Supremes. (And they too are from Detroit.) But a solo career after a lifetime of duet is daunting. And I'm more scared than excited—of everything these days. Plus, I'm running out of money. Again.

My weekend-receptionist tenure comes to a close, and I take a waitressing job at Baby Bo's Burritos. This, along with the bulk mailings, makes up the majority of my income. There are two things that make me particularly good at waitressing. One, I remember people—and what they order—from night to night, week to week. I can call them by name and recite their culinary likes and dislikes. I even make friends. And two, I have a gift for back talk. When one customer reaches out to grab my elbow in some lame attempt to get attention, I turn and say, "We don't touch our waitresses in New York." And when another, drunk out of his mind, proclaims that he wants to fuck me, I say, without missing a beat, "Well, I don't want to fuck you. And I'm working." I've heard that "if you want self-esteem, do self-estimable acts," and I believe this is so. Working steady jobs, earning enough money to actually live on, breaking free of my mom and her credit cards brings a surge of power and confidence. The fear lessens its grip.

This is when writing becomes a regular part of my life. I've kept a journal since I was sixteen and have written fiction intermittently since college—a short story at Barnard, a few monologues in Providence, and even an eight-page play. But now I write every day. And I perform my auto-biographical "solo theater" pieces (a friend calls them "Sit-down Stand-up") however and wherever I can. I book myself as a writer/performer into clubs, cafés, bars, even living rooms as part of a "salon series" that a friend and I curate. I join a feedback group for independent perform-ing artists through a young arts organization called The Field. We meet weekly to show one another work and offer critiques, and at the end of a ten-week session, perform for the public in a small theater in SoHo. Eventually this leads to the formation of a group called Solo 5, in which five solo performance artists (including me) commit to work-ing in cocreative models. At first we produce one another's solo work—like a collective—and then we start investigating how to weave the solos together into evening-length group pieces. Outside of Solo 5, I'm investigating how to make these pieces bigger, which I start to think might mean inviting other performers onstage with me, which just might lead to writing plays. As an experiment, to see if I am actually capable of this endeavor, I write a twenty-page play called *The Dead End of Magic*. I bring scenes into my feedback group once a week and eventually produce the piece in The Field's "90 Plays in 9 Days" festival. We perform for one night at a rented theater downtown—shared light plot, basic design elements, do-it-yourself costumes—and it's bliss. My friend Douglas directs and a number of my other friends act in the play, which is about a twenty-something virgin who lives in SoHo, finds magic playing cards on the street, and loves a boy who can't/won't love her back. You might say it was autobiographical. And you might be right.

I start dressing like a grunge girl or, rather, like a grunge boy with tits: Oversized plaid flannel shirts. Jeans with holes worn over tights. Combat boots. Sometimes little flowery skirts over the tights and combat boots. I paint bold streaks into my brown hair—gold and orange and black. I cut tiny bangs—like Audrey Hepburn in *Roman Holiday*—with nail scissors. And I write about everything and everyone I meet.

At the beginning of 1992, after roughly six months of living together, Margot announces that she will be moving out. That same week I'm having dinner with my friend Sarah, who bemoans living at home with her parents while saving up enough money for a first apartment. I invite Sarah to move in. Perfect!

Sarah and I met at theater camp at Northwestern University when we were both seventeen and have been friends ever since. I visited her in Manhattan during the fateful trip when I told my mom, "I'm looking at colleges and staying with friends. Don't call me, I'll call you." We recemented the friendship in Providence, while she was at Brown and I was at Trinity Rep. She is one of my dear friends—her birthday three days apart from mine—and from the first she is the best thing to happen to 101 Thompson.

For one thing, she decorates. She brings fresh flowers into the house and a set of her mother's (matching floral) dishes. She calls Marc the Hot Landlord and convinces him to pay for fancy tiles, which she picks out from a nearby Italian design store, for our kitchen. And then Sarah and her mother go to IKEA, which has recently opened in Elizabeth, New Jersey, and buy a kitchen table, bedroom furniture for her, and necessary kitchen things for us both. I realize this is how healthy mothers behave. They are able to come and take their daughters shopping. My mother would like nothing better, but she's stuck with her semiparalyzed husband. And although she offers to send me a TV every chance she gets ("a really small one, for your kitchen"), I don't really watch TV. So I always say no. She rarely asks what I do need, but honestly, my mom has her hands full, and I don't want to fight.

Another thing about Sarah: She comes with a social life. We've always had friends in common, first from theater camp and then from Providence, but now individual friends become a cohesive community. And I have a crush on an actor named Sam whose roommate has a crush on Sarah, and so there are double dates spent watching *Saturday Night Live* and eating ice cream on the boys' secondhand couch.

In October 1992 Marilyn is turning fifty, and I suggest

she spend her birthday in New York. Despite her addiction to luxury hotels, she agrees to stay with me, and I'm excited to host her, to share where I live, how I live, and how nice it is. Sarah goes to her boyfriend's, I take her room, and we give Marilyn mine.

When my mom gets out of the cab I'm surprised. A year of caring for the sick Archduke has taken its toll. She looks great—little black DKNY dress, short spiky wheat-colored blond hair—but she can barely walk down the street. Her eyesight is failing, and her feet hurt—perhaps from the vastly inappropriate shoes she's brought or perhaps from the diabetes. It's hard to tell.

I plan a weekend full of cultural events. On her birthday, we go to the Magritte exhibit at the Metropolitan Museum of Art and the next night to a concert at Carnegie Hall. We visit places I think she will like—a West Village café named after the composer Vivaldi, and to the Cupping Room and shopping. We even host a brunch so that she can meet my friends. There are a few good moments—my favorite, in the Metropolitan Museum, when Marilyn stands in front of an African fertility sculpture exclaiming, "They sure could make tits." But on the whole, the visit exhausts us both. For one thing, she doesn't feel well and can't walk for very long without getting tired. For another, an eerie confrontation is taking place inside my mom between the younger woman she once was and the fifty-year-old she is today. She is no longer the center of attention because of her outrageous beauty. And this is neither comfortable nor easy. She wants to be the Marilyn who came to New York with Harvey, stayed at The Regency, ate at the best restaurants, shopped in the best shops, went to see Joan Rivers at Upstairs at the Downstairs ("Honey, are you still on the

Pill?" Joan would ask my mom, in the audience) and Bobby
Short at the Café Carlyle. She wants to know the best places,
be given the best tables, and shop at all of her once-favorite
boutiques. But she is no longer that person. Present-day
Marilyn is a fifty-year-old Midwesterner in a bad marriage
with a semiparalyzed old person. And this kills her.

When she leaves, I spiral into doubt, confusion, and
depression. This will become typical of most contact with
my mother over the next decade. For about two weeks
after her visit, I am infected by a formless and insidious
sadness—it pervades everything I do. Daily activities are
unusually anxiety provoking, overwhelming. I become
intensely emotional in unpredictable ways. And I start
spending money. Little things. A dinner here and there.
On her credit cards. My therapist calls this "survivor guilt."
I am physically healthy and financially solvent, neither of
which can be said of my mother. Marilyn's magic powers
are beginning to wane, mine are on the rise, and the whole
thing makes me feel sick inside.

But soon I have other things to think about. An
eight-page play I've written has been accepted for production by Naked Angels, a fresh young theater company made
up of movie stars who work out of a loft on Seventeenth
Street. My professional debut as a writer is about to occur.

I start meeting with the fancy director from the fancy
theater company, going to breakfast and talking about
rewrites (on an eight-page play!). There are two important
things to note here. One, everyone else participating in
this event is some kind of celebrity. So while all of the project participants are working for free, without a contract, it
is not a level playing field. They don't need the money. I,

on the other hand, start missing waitressing shifts in order
to go to rehearsal, which means I'm losing money and
struggling. Second, and perhaps more important, I have
no idea what playwrights actually *do*. I go to rehearsal every
day, and they ask me questions that I can't answer because
at this point my entire process is "intuitive." I am winging
it. Badly. Between the financial stress and the artistic stress,
I am not sleeping and literally pulling my hair out. My chi-
ropractor/naturopath, Heidi, puts me on a flower essence
called Rock Rose meant to treat extreme terror, children
who wake up in the middle of the night still in the grip of
nightmares.

I stop attending rehearsal for a week thinking, "let go."
But at the final dress rehearsal I discover that the actresses
have started making up lines of their own and adding them
to my play. Letting go didn't work. Horrified, I protest.
One of the great joys of playwriting is that the writer maintains copyright, owning her work after any given production. Changes cannot be made to the text without the
writer's permission. When the director of my eight-minute
play asks, "What's your bottom line?" I'm caught off guard.
I'm twenty-three and have no idea what a "bottom line" IS.
Coached by a former teacher, I say, "The actresses have to
speak every word of text as written." And, blessedly, she
agrees. By the time the play is on its feet, running—for a
whole month!—I'm determined to write another and this
time do it right.

I start attending Naked Angels' now-infamous Tuesdays
at Nine—evenings devoted to the development of new work.
Each week writers brings in ten pages of dialogue, hand
the pages to actors selected at random, and then everyone

performs the work without any rehearsal. It's a great laboratory to see if something will "play." Writers at every level
show up—from the established (Kenneth Lonergan) to the
emerging (Jonathan Marc Sherman) to the naive and clue-
less (me). And this is where and how I start teaching myself
to be a playwright.

During this period, Sarah gets a promotion and decides
it's time to try living alone. I'm devastated when she moves
out, but we promise to stay in touch. The teary good-bye
is funny when we acknowledge that she's only going two
blocks away, to Thompson and Bleecker. Still, it feels big.
A young art student moves in, and although she will never
be the friend and sister that Sarah is, we do all right. Soon,
though, I start to wonder if I too can make enough money
to live on my own. Farther down Thompson, near Grand, I
hear studios are going for something like $800. I try to imag-
ine the increase—from 550 to 800-plus bills, which would
no longer be shared. But I can't see it. The gap between what I
want and what I feel I can have or earn is just too big. I remind
myself that the real goal, always, is to be a self-supporting
artist who can live within her means. Living alone will have
to wait. "Baby steps," I remind myself. The dream is being
lived. A play is in production and another is being written. It's
all going as planned.

And then, in June 1993, the whole thing falls apart.

It is June 8, 1993, and I'm walking home from rehearsing a new solo piece based on the myth of Persephone
and Demeter. Persephone, it has been explained to me, is
dragged into the underworld and raped, but at the end of
the story achieves autonomy from a dominant (goddess)
mother. She becomes a queen (of the underworld) and

one of the only characters in Greek mythology to travel freely between the world of the living and the world of the dead. I've become obsessed with this tale, as if Persephone's time in hell might justify how hard I've found it to leave my mom and forge a separate identity. What I don't expect is just how closely interwoven our stories will be.

The main thing is, I walk home that night feeling satisfied. I'm scheduled to perform the piece in roughly ten days, and I think I'll be ready. Maybe I stop into Merchants, a local bar, to see if my friend Tina is drinking martinis. Maybe when I can't find her, I stay anyway, joining some theater people I know who've just come back from a wedding in Vermont. Maybe I stay and have a soda. (I still don't drink alcohol. That's about to change, too.) And maybe I walk home—with my friend Ken all the way to Houston— feeling happy, connected, alive. My new roommate is in Cherry Hill, New Jersey, so when I get home, I have the place to myself. The roommate has taken the window guards off the window in her room, but I never go into her room without her, so I may not be aware of the fact that there is an open window—on a fire escape, without window barriers—when I go to sleep, just after midnight.

I open my eyes at 4 A.M. to find a stranger in a black Lone Ranger mask standing at the foot of my bed. The man is of indiscriminate race (Italian? Mexican? Middle Eastern? He's not black, he's not brown, he's not exactly white—he's sort of swarthy, and I don't even know what that word means until I see this man) and of medium height and medium build. He wears a black turtleneck (in June in New York City, for God's sake) and black pants and the aforementioned mask. And he's just standing there, watching me, not saying a word. Immediately I apprehend what is about to happen, and all I can say is, "Please don't hurt me."

I'm twenty-four years old, I'm a virgin, and I'm being raped by a stranger who looks like an existentialist Zorro on Halloween. For one split second I think, This can't happen to me because I'm very smart. I write plays in which I deconstruct sexuality and make fun of my own virginity. I'm a twenty-four-year-old virgin! Like the Virgin Mary. You can't rape the Virgin Mary.

But he does.

And then the most amazing thing happens. It sounds ludicrous (and, yes, I was in shock) but I feel like I'm being lifted out of my body and enveloped in light. I know that I am stronger than the rapist. I know that I will live. I know that he's in more pain than I am. And I know—without question—that I'm protected, held in the arms of the Divine. I am going to survive this night.

And I do.

When the man leaves, I am still. I can't tell whether he's still in the apartment, but I imagine myself a deer, and I use my deer senses to tell me when it's safe to run. I run through the hallway of my building, naked from the waist down, the pajamas he's used to gag me still hanging around my neck, and I start banging on doors, demanding that someone help me.

And they do.

Strangers on the fifth floor let me into their apartment and give me a pair of shorts to wear. They call 911. And then I call Grace, who's mercifully living in New York that summer while completing an internship. She comes immediately. The paramedics and Grace take me to St. Vincent's emergency room, and my sweet friend says, "You're not going back to that apartment." And she takes me home with her, to 11 Waverly (which, it's not lost on me, is also the title of Ethan Hawke's first novel). And then, because we don't know what else to do, and we need somebody's mommy, if not mine, she takes me to her parents' house and that's when we talk about where I'm going to live.

Grace feels very strongly that I cannot ever go back to 101 Thompson.

"Ever?" I ask.

"You can go back there to pack. But not by yourself."

Grateful that someone is telling me what to do, I do not go back to that apartment. Except to pack. And even then, as Grace has promised, never alone.

I spend a few nights with Grace and her boyfriend in the one-room apartment on Waverly and the rest of that first week shuttling between friends. Nobody has a guest room, and only one person I know has a couch, but her roommate won't let me stay on it for more than a night, so I am left wondering, *Now what?* I have no savings account, and the deposit, which Marc the Hot Landlord will refund to me, won't cover first month and last month's rent on a new apartment. Nobody in my family can help me. My mom is still slightly hysterical (although, to her credit, she's bought a few books on rape-crisis trauma and sought out someone to talk to). My grandmother sends a purple terry cloth robe. And when I finally ask for help, my mother's sister sends $200, which affords me two weeks' time off from work, and that's about it. I am, as they say, shit out of luck. Until my new friend Bryan, a sweet gay man who I've started to go dancing with, offers an alcove in the back of his Brooklyn Heights apartment. He says, "Stay with me and my roommate for as long as you need." And so, by the end of June, I am living on Pierrepont Street in Brooklyn Heights, in a three-sided room with no fourth wall, and I have no idea what to do next.

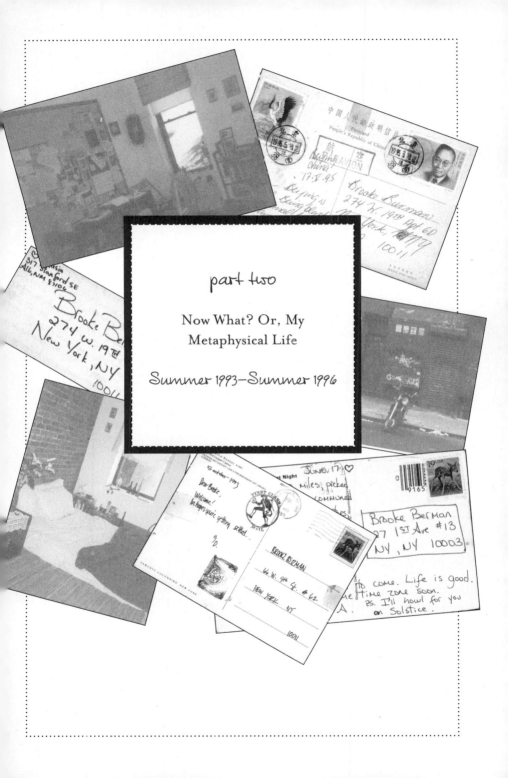

part two

Now What? Or, My
Metaphysical Life

Summer 1993–Summer 1996

48 Pierrepont Street, Brooklyn

Living at Bryan's has its charm, despite the dire circumstances. For one thing, the apartment is huge: a spacious floor-through with two and a half bedrooms (guess who has the half?) and an enormous bright living room on the top floor of a brownstone in one of the best neighborhoods in Brooklyn. Bryan has made it design-magazine beautiful. A food and wine person, he has ensured that the best part of the house is his kitchen. And then there's Brooklyn Heights itself, charming and quaint with a "promenade" and benches along the waterfront. Perfect for reflection, for peace of mind. I walk over the bridge into Manhattan on a regular basis (often an attempt to save subway fare but also an aesthetic perk of the neighborhood). But the charm wears thin when I remember I can't stay here indefinitely. There's no one taking care of me. I have to earn money and find a place to live by the end of the summer. Bryan and his roommate haven't said as much—in fact, they are nothing but generous during the entire three months I live with them—but it's clear nonetheless. This is a Band-Aid, not a permanent measure.

"Healing" from the rape is a mysterious proposition. How can I heal from something that I can't see, something that has left no physical mark or scar? I'm a good girl, and I do as I'm told. I meet with the rape-crisis counselor at St. Vincent's, with my therapist, and with Heidi, the chiropractor I've been seeing regularly since 1992 when I threw my neck out dancing at the Crow Bar. It was Heidi, along with my therapist, who urged me to tell my mother about the attack. Initially, I had wanted to protect Marilyn (and maybe myself) from the horrible news, but both psychologist and intuitive chiropractor agreed, "She needs to know." Now, Heidi encourages me to draw pictures and journal, to take long hot baths in essential oils with the goal of helping my spirit come back into my body and feel safe there. I do all of the above. But no one has anything more tangible to say, except the friend who tells me straight out, "No one can make this better." This is really the best piece of advice I could get because up until now I've been waiting for someone to do just that. And they're all waiting for me. Not one therapist, peer counselor, social worker, body worker, naturopath, or acupuncture guru has any germane piece of wisdom or advice besides, *it takes time.* And the thing is, I don't (yet) feel particularly traumatized by the rape. Instead, I identify my trauma as specifically about housing. I have lost my home. I need a home. I don't know how to find a home. I walk around the Heights most nights alone, feeling traumatized not by sexual violence but by real estate and money. The friend who says I can't be helped is right—because I want to be rescued. Rescue is not forthcoming.

I work all summer at a catering job for the Chelsea-based Beauty and the Feast. I have the very good fortune of being included in the circle of an actor named Michael who is both generous and entrepreneurial, and keeps all of his friends apprised of job opportunities. I don't know how he does it, but Michael always knows the best and most innovative part-time jobs, and he is always hooking us up. So a group of actors and writers who sort of loosely know one another through Michael show up daily at Beauty and the Feast where we are handed enormous picnic baskets full of overpriced gourmet sandwiches. We're given a "route," much like a paper route, and we hawk our wares. The best part: We're allowed to take home whatever goes unsold. The job pays decently enough, and the food keeps me going all summer: White bean pâté. Thai chicken wraps. Fusilli with sun-dried tomato in tiny plastic Beauty and the Feast containers. By the end of June, I have fallen into a routine and many things—at least the external things—fall into place.

Other things, like peace of mind and casual interactions, will take longer. One night, at a local bodega, a teenager in pants four sizes too big for him makes a lewd comment about my butt. When I ignore him, he says, "Bitch won't talk to me because I'm black." To which I say, "Actually, it's because I got raped by a stranger last month, and I'm still freaked out." Silence. And then the kid says, "I'm sorry. That happened to my sister. Are you okay?" And we share a real moment. "Is your sister okay?" I ask. Again I am told it takes time.

But here's the thing about time. Although it's passing, reminding me daily that summer is coming to an end and I still have no real plans, it doesn't seem to be doing much for my state of mind or feelings of general well-being. The passing of time makes me more and more desperate to find some sort of resolve that I do not yet have. At night, alone in the little alcove room, I think, *Someday, someone will love me, and I will tell him all about this summer . . . and his love will erase the horror and loneliness.* And then I wait.

On the Fourth of July I take a trip to Detroit to see

Marilyn. On the day after the rape, when I finally called to tell her what had happened, I was strict. I said, "Mommy, here's the thing. You can't cry right now, I haven't cried yet. And I can't take care of you. So you're going to have to find someone else to cry with so that you can be strong for me." (To her credit, she did.) A month later I feel ready to see her. I tell myself that it will be good for us, and also that I can handle whatever emotional peril she feels that my experience has placed her in. I even bring presents—a mug from Pottery Barn and a picture frame for my grandmother. But I'm not ready. I'm still raw. And ill-equipped to take care of my mom or her projections about safety and violation. I realize this almost immediately. Marilyn wants to be good to me, to help and take care of me; she wants to take anything that has had the power to hurt me far far away. But her own fears are too big, and she doesn't know what to *do*. We fight. She can't undo the fact of this terrible thing that has happened or the senseless guilt that somehow it was her job to prevent it, to keep me safe. You can't keep your daughter safe when she lives across the country. But you're not supposed to, I try to tell her. At some point, part of mothering must include letting go, trusting your child to find her way, trusting the Universe or Life Force or Deity to protect her when you cannot. Even when your daughter gets hurt.

The counselor at St. Vincent's has said, "Rape unleashes many women's deepest fears about their own safety, about being female." I can see this now, with my mom. The word itself is not part of her vocabulary, and its associations bring up primal responses. Marilyn takes me to get a manicure, a pedicure, and a makeover. But she can't talk about the actual event or say the word "rape." Maybe she is afraid.

Maybe she doesn't want to probe or upset me, maybe she and my grandmother feel some kind of shame or fear of what they imagine to be my shame. But I am not ashamed. And it goes undiscussed, which, in the end, upsets me more. I don't want a makeover—I don't feel ugly or dirty—I want to talk about what happened.

When I get back to New York, I have a chiropractic adjustment scheduled and, in Heidi's office, I break down sobbing. I let it all out, howling—full-on, full-bodied, full-voice—as if there is no end to the pain. It is the first time since the rape that I've allowed myself to do so. Heidi welcomes me to spend the afternoon in her office, and then she refers me to another healer, Ross, who she says "can help." When I meet Ross a week later, she insists I slow down and befriend the Void. Ross says, "You're so committed to *not* being a victim—but what about acknowledging that you were hurt?" She calls the entire experience "an initiation." And it helps to think of it that way.

In the "initiation" paradigm, an event or a crisis comes in to shatter the preconceptions and ego structure of the initiate, forcing him or her to let go of the smaller container and smaller definitions and become larger. This "larger" includes taking on more of his or her soul and soul identity. Eventually, the initiate will help others through the same process. Ross prescribes spending time in the Void every day—listening, breathing, feeling, receiving. Rather than use my intellect to force solutions or find answers that don't really exist for me yet, she suggests that I sit with the not-knowing and build internal strength and substance. She's right. When I slow down, the feelings are more manageable and less intense. When I temper my impulse to immediately process and be done with something, I am forced to wait. But waiting is good! As the Tao says, "Practice not-doing, and everything will fall into place." It says, "The Tao is . . . like the eternal void . . . filled with infinite possibilities." Waiting is uncomfortable—the ego likes solutions, plans, time frames, and promises—but necessary.

By August, without any real plan or direction, I decide to move out of 48 Pierrepont. Bryan and his roommate have never once asked me to go. The most they've done is to ask, politely and only lately, what my plans are. But I don't have any—I really just want to live with them and be taken care of—and so I feel compelled to invent some. I call my mother's best friend, a married teacher in Maryland whom I have always liked, and ask if I might visit her. In some version of the fantasy, maybe I think I'll stay there, move in, be her kid, and get a job in Potomac. She says that I am welcome to visit for as long as I like. I pack my things and go.

....

Maryland
Then quickly back to New York:
309 East 9th Street
274 West 72nd Street

Maryland is awkward. It's no one's fault. My mom's friend and her kids are fabulous. The house is big and nestled into the woods. And everyone wants to be good to me. But I can't escape myself. And I really, really want to. I move on quickly, after just one week. I need a place where I can unravel, stare at the walls, be in whatever kind of mood I want without the pressure of social interaction. I need a home. And New York is still my best bet.

Back in the city, I have arranged a house-sitting gig with my friend Lisa, a red-haired actress whom I've known since Providence. Lisa is visiting her family in San Diego for a few weeks, and I am relieved to have my own place in the East Village again—a 1BR apartment above a scarf and trinket shop, across from Veselka and just a few doors west of the puppet artist's place where I house-sat three years earlier. Something I both love and hate about Manhattan is that its geography is limited—an island—and therefore circular. You can't escape your past. I find myself spending three weeks on the same block as the place in which I stayed, for about the same amount of time, three years earlier. I think this is a homing device. East Ninth Street likes me as much as I like it. Maybe I belong here. It's ridiculously hot in late August, and Lisa has no AC, but I want to stay forever. And again, forever is not an option.

I start looking at shares again: Brooklyn, Manhattan, DUMBO (an area "Down Under the Manhattan Bridge Overpass"—on the edge of Brooklyn Heights—it will be superchic in ten years, full of art galleries and fancy stores and restaurants, but in 1993 it's rough and a little dangerous). Within a week or two I find a place, through a friend—a share in the West Village—but the room won't be available until October 1, which leaves me homeless for just about one month. Although I am sure that Bryan and his roommate would be amenable to one more month, something prevents me from calling them. In fact, once I move out of their place, the friendships die pretty quickly. It's my own fault. I still don't want to be seen as a victim. I don't want to know anyone who knows me as a victim. I just want to keep moving.

I spend the month of September—for free—in the apartment of a girl I've met through my weekly acting class. Mandy, a few years older than me, has a spacious 1BR in a doorman building on the Upper West Side. She says she's mostly living with her boyfriend but can't bear to give up her own place and invites me over to take a look. There are more scented candles and floral throw pillows than I ever imagined possible. But it's centrally located, and free, and I have no other offers. Mandy invites me to move in for the month, while I'm in between places, and aware of the reasons I've been semi-lost all summer, she buys me a book called *The Heroine's Journey*. The book, by a Jungian family therapist, offers a "feminine" map of healing, suggesting that women's spiritual initiations always involve a trip into the darkness, something akin to rape, either psychic or physical. Years later, when studying Kabbalah, I will hear something like this again. The vessel is shattered in order to be rebuilt and ultimately contain more of the initiate's true essence, which is Divine. It's a great book. And now, for one more month, I have the space I need. Until Mandy and her boyfriend break up, and she moves back in. And now, she jokes, she needs the book back. But it's all okay. Because as soon as October 1 rolls around, I am moving to the West Village.

....

66 West 9th Street

The apartment on West Ninth is a corner 2BR on the sixth floor of an old building. Its windows (including a curved window seat in the living room!) look out over lower Sixth Avenue and a public library, which used to be a women's prison, and neighboring gardens. The location is amazing, the views are remarkable, and the rent is miraculously low. We're paying, between the two of us, $1,085 a month. Again, because my room is smaller, my rent is less. I pay $485, which I can *just* afford.

"Tiny" does not begin to describe this room. If I thought any of my previous rooms were small, I must have been mistaken because this one takes the proverbial cake. It holds a twin-size futon and the board-and-crate desk configuration from Thompson Street. Nothing more. (Added perk: an antique built-in closet, my favorite part of the entire apartment.) It is perfect for me. Something about the break-in and rape, now four months behind me, have made small spaces attractive. There's no room for anyone to hide, nothing in the room that I can't see and touch.

Male roommates are also attractive. And now I have one. Matt, a dancer and a Virgo, has recently returned from a spiritual retreat where he started meditating and gave up dairy products. The week I move in, he takes it upon himself to alphabetize my cassette collection while I'm out, displaying the entire thing proudly on the bookshelf in the living room. I'm horrified. As an only child, to me, "my" means my. I quickly unalphabetize the whole thing, so that I can find what I need in the way I like (by genre, not alphabetized by artist's last name). Years later, I'll run into Matt at a dance concert in Chelsea and feel remorse, wishing that we had become friends. But in 1993 friendship is not on the playlist. Something about Matt demands to be paid attention to at all times. It's nothing he's doing on purpose (although he does like to blast Sting's "Fields of Gold" at full volume first thing in the morning). Maybe it's his height or his booming voice or his energy, which naturally expands to fill whatever space he is in—but Matt is way too much for me.

Still, I'm excited to live with a guy, not to mention a guy with a spiritual practice. And the move itself is easy. I've hired my friends Rainn and Holly from Beauty and the Feast. Rainn (who will grow up to become Rainn Wilson) is an unemployed actor with a van. He and Holly have started the Transcendent Moving Company. I pay them forty bucks an hour plus gas, and they and a few friends and I spend the day gathering my belongings, which are scattered in a number of places around Manhattan and Brooklyn. I have suitcases at Mandy's, plus eight boxes at Bryan's in Brooklyn Heights, and the rest (my dresser, a mirror, more boxes) stored in Bryan's mom's basement in Great Neck. The move takes all day. And then, once we've unloaded everything on Ninth Street, we eat pizza in the new apartment. This will later become a moving day ritual: Gather as many friends as possible, find someone with a van, and buy them all pizza and beer when the work is complete.

Now it is time to shop. My mother urges me to take her American Express card to Bed Bath & Beyond to buy new towels and sheets, a duvet, and whatever else I need to "feel at home." I am happy to oblige. If my twin-size futon is tiny (*monastic*, I think, with romantic visions of writing a masterpiece from this cozy room in the West Village), it will at least be well outfitted. I buy beautiful soft Egyptian cotton sheets and throw pillows. Everything is white and pale aqua, like the ocean on another planet, designed to soothe my soul and heal the memory of interrupted sleep. Only

I can't sleep. Soon after moving in, without any warning, I start to wake up at 4 A.M. The time the rape occurred. Every morning.

Up until now, I've slept without difficulty. One nightmare the whole summer. (It took place in a postapocalyptic New York that resembled, oddly, the set for the NYU production of *Angels in America* starring Debra Messing. And indeed, an angel, in the dream, rescued me and carried me away and out of the burning city.) Now, suddenly, I can fall asleep—but I can't stay asleep for very long. At the 4 A.M. marker, as if an alarm has sounded, I open my eyes, expecting to see a stranger. Every single morning. And every single morning I go through the trial and error of, *what do I do?* Counting sheep doesn't work. Reading makes me anxious. I don't own a TV set, and I don't want to buy one. I become intimate with the dawn and predawn hours, the sky over Sixth Avenue from our living room window. Eventually, I decide not to try to force anything. If I can't sleep, I will turn on the light. I will color, write, draw, make tea. I will not make myself stay in bed. Or close my eyes. And I strike deals. For instance, for safety, I have to stay in the apartment, but if I'm still awake at sunrise, I can go to the nearby twenty-four-hour bistro, French Roast, for a 5 A.M. breakfast. In this hot spot that caters to downtown hipsters and Ethan Hawke, the 5 A.M. crowd is different—more truckers than disaffected youth. I bring my journal and write until sunrise while drinking enormous bowls of café au lait. I learn to turn something terrible into something palatable, if not sustainable.

While my nights are defined by trauma and the promise of French Roast, my days are defined by unrequited crushes and lack of funds. I've quit both Beauty and the Feast and the waitressing job. I'm still doing mailings at Dance Theater Workshop, something I can do without being visible, hiding in big clothes in the back "studio" where the mailing table lives. But apart from that, I have been too sensitive, my emotions too much of a wild card to hold steady work. I don't want to spend my nights in restaurants with drunk people or my days walking around the city with lunch baskets. I tell myself I don't want any aspect of my daily life to be unexamined or unwanted. But sensitivity comes with a price—I'm hard up for cash. Once again, I put out a call to everyone I know and, once again, I say yes to every job that comes my way. The one that sticks is with the Princeton Review, the organization known for preparing students to take SAT exams.

This job is a perfect fit. I proctor practice exams for LSAT students who meet twice a week at the College of Insurance in TriBeCa (dangerously close to the new apartment of my Finance Guy ex). I arrive early to set up the rooms and administer the two- to three-hour instrument of pre—law school torture. The best part is, my friend Melinda, who got me the job, proctors the exam in the room next door. In between sections, while the students are taking their tests, Melinda and I meet in the hallway for twenty-five- to forty-minute gossip breaks. On the days that I give actual exams (Saturdays in Brooklyn Heights), when Melinda isn't around, I take my notebooks and write. "You have fifteen minutes" and "Turn to the next section" become phrases I can utter in my sleep. If I were sleeping.

I start a relationship with an actor. As we walk through the annual Halloween parade, Jake, twenty-seven and recently divorced, says the only kind of relationship he can have is "solely sexual." I suggest that we try "soul-ly sexual" but he is unconvinced. And I'm still a virgin—albeit now a virgin rape survivor who doesn't sleep past 4 A.M.— so, obviously, nothing is going to be "solely sexual." After some back and forth (and some really good coffee and make-out sessions) we part. I spend Thanksgiving with Melinda and her older sister at a chic restaurant in SoHo— Cosmopolitans and smashed potatoes—feeling sorry for myself, thinking, *I will be alone forever.* And then I get a troubling message. Sam, of the *Saturday Night Live* couch-dates, has checked himself into the psych ward of New York Hospital.

Sam has always been a superhero to me, tall and lanky, beautiful and brilliant—Captain America with twinkling eyes. We met at Sarah's twenty-first birthday party when all three of us were living in Providence. At the party, he stood next to the two birthday cakes (one lemon and one chocolate) as if he were an appointed official offering insights into which was better (the lemon) and why (its frosting). I started a conversation with him thinking, This is the most beautiful male person I have ever seen. A week later, he ushered for *The Obscene Bird of Night,* the play I was performing downtown at Trinity Rep. My costume in said play consisted of a blue garter belt, an enormous black bra, and a blond bouffant wig, and the reviewers referred to me as "a butterball of fun," which made me think I was fat. Sam and I walked home together that night talking about Walt Whitman and indie rock. I was smitten.

In 1992, we reconnected in New York and became friends. The first night we hung out, after hours of roaming around SoHo discussing poetry and music and life, he took me to my front door and said, "Am I supposed to kiss you good night? Because I have a girlfriend in Paris ... and I've really just never had a good platonic female friend." His voice was so sincere, and his eyes were so beautiful. I said, "Don't kiss me good night. We're going to be good, good friends." Soon we were. Sam and I hung out in each other's apartments, watched TV, saw plays, cared for each other over respective heartbreaks, and I gave him my work to read. Sam was the only male friend who wasn't freaked out by the information that I'd been raped, who knew unquestionably how to show up. He phoned right away, "What can I do for you?" So when Sam's girlfriend calls to tell me that he's in trouble, I'm there.

I visit Sam in the psych ward at New York Hospital the Monday after Thanksgiving. According to his girlfriend, he'd lost a job, become increasingly anxious, and started to think dark thoughts, resulting in a typical psychotic episode— the kind in which one hears voices, believes the President is communicating through the TV set, and the neighbors are listening in through the walls. It was Sam's choice to check himself into a hospital. He was afraid of hurting himself and didn't know what else to do.

The first time that I visit—a journey that will become rote, the 6 train to 68th Street/Hunter College, a long walk east—I think, *This is what we do for each other. Police stations, emergency rooms, rape-crisis centers, psych wards. This is just what we do.*

The Payne Whitney Clinic has its own separate entrance. When visiting, I am asked to sign a register and state my relationship to the patient. And then I am given a visitors sticker to attach to my clothes, and a pass to the elevator. On Sam's floor, I have to ring the bell and be let in by a staff member behind the locked door. It's high security. A nurse points me down the hallway to my friend's room. He seems happy to see me—as does his girlfriend, who's been holding down the fort all weekend, mostly by herself. I spend as much time as I can trying to understand what has happened, absorb it, listen to both of their accounts of the episode itself and the days leading up to it. It is, as I will later learn, classic: *The aliens are coming, the cities will burn, everything has meaning and then double secret meaning . . . and I have a mission . . . to save the world. . . . Only nobody will listen and the mission is incomplete, but the pressure is mounting. These are the final days.*

And then the weirdest thing happens. As he is talking, I start to see light encircling my sedated and frightened friend. Light shoots out of Sam's head, surrounding him like a halo or an aura. His face grows close and then far, changing in the light, transmuting until all I can see is hypnotic bright white light.

I don't say a word about it. Sam keeps talking. I keep listening. I can't imagine interupting him to say, "Hey, um, I see light shooting out of your head." In fact, it would mirror the very things he's most afraid of. I would sound as crazy as him, and then where would we be? But it is a gorgeous display, not unlike the light that enfolded me the night I was raped. This makes me think that Sam and I are on the same path. He's being protected—and initiated—too.

His girlfriend tells me that the night Sam checked himself in, the doctors asked, "Do you think you're in touch with reality?"

And Sam said, "I went to Brown. We were taught that reality is subjective."

It's my favorite story these days.

I visit a few times in early December. He's still sedated and scared but that same light is in his eyes, and when he tells me the things he's afraid of, and the psychotic visions he's had, he makes sense. In fact, his visions and fears sound a lot like the things I've been hearing from healers. I don't think he's crazy; I think he's waking up. All of the spiritual teachings and New Age manifestos I've been reading say: *The old world is breaking down, and a new one will rise in its place. We are here to bring the new world into manifestation.* So I ignore the parts of Sam's narrative that include fire in the streets and aliens and focus instead on the light in his eyes and the light I still see surrounding him. He is like me. We are part of a wave of transformation.

What I don't yet see is that by helping Sam I'm helping myself. I need what he does: nurture, care, rest, time, and patience. I don't know how to give those things to myself. But I do know how to give them to him. So I give. And this provides a focus, respite from my own pain and the fear of what will come next. And the world gets colder, and the Christmas holidays get nearer, and one night, heading uptown to a friend's holiday party, I lose my shit. I'm on the subway, Sony Sports Walkman in my ears, listening to a band called The Story, a song from a mother's point of view. The singer, Jonatha Brooke, croons, "You were so much, so much mine, now I reach for you and I cannot find you . . ." Although I've heard this song before—many, many times—tonight it hits a nerve. I feel what Marilyn must have the morning I called to tell her I'd been raped. Considering a mother's love, the kind of protection a mother

wants to envision for her child, and the profound sense
of powerlessness when her child gets hurt—and remembering Marilyn's own powerlessness—it's all too much. I'd
want to hold my daughter immediately, the way my mother
must have wanted to hold me. This is the first time I can
acknowledge the very basic truth: I got hurt. Up until now,
I'd been feeling "inviolate." An initiate. Strong and brave.
And during the rape itself I'd had that vision, where I was
held in the arms of the Divine, encircled by light, stronger
than the rapist. But now I feel something else: *I am vulnerable
and I got hurt.* This thought slices me open. I start sobbing.
The New York subway system is not a great place to feel
sliced open or even vulnerable. I need to get out of town.
Pronto.

I arrange to spend a few weeks in the Berkshires with
friends—dancers I've known since my DTW internship,
who'd given up trying to "make it" and instead decided to
make something else, something wholesome and nour-
ishing, outside of New York City. Jeannie and Rae and
Connor and Dave have all moved away and set up house in
Northampton, Massachusetts, where they teach "authentic movement," cook vegan food, and try to live as if in
an ideal world (or, at least, a more humane one). They
press me, Why do I stay in New York City? And I can't
answer them. The truth is, I can't imagine leaving. Where
would I go? Would I come here? They haven't invited me
to move in, so what are we talking about? I try to imagine a life in Northampton, with its sweet musty-smelling
used-bookstore-cafés and artistic community. I imagine
moving into Rae's attic or renting a room in a house somewhere, like Grace did after dropping out of Hampshire.
I'd wear a lot of layers, eat organic food, and go to "open

movement" workshops. But is that my path? Or does it just
look good because a group of my friends are doing it? And
honestly—layers notwithstanding—isn't this what I do in
New York?

I insist New York is home. There is something I love and
crave about its energy. The City grounds me. Why would
I leave? And I still want to be a working artist, even when
Jeannie and Rae insist, "You have to get off the career path!
It's killing you! You're dragging your soul around!" I still
want to make a life as a full-time paid professional artist in
the theater. And I don't see why I have to sacrifice that in
order to "heal" my "soul." What if the work I do brings me
to my soul? What if it is my soul? Can't we have souls and
careers both? Besides, I tell Rae, with some defensive edge,
"My creative life in the city is rich." I don't even know that's
true until I say it, and then I must admit it is.

When I get back to Ninth Street, I devote myself to
Sam's recovery. After all, we're both trafficking in light
beams and nothing else makes sense. My work schedule
allows for this since the mailings at DTW can happen on
my own schedule (I have keys) and the Princeton Review
shifts are only twice a week. I have plenty of time to sit in
the hospital with my friend. On his rare passes, permission
to leave the building, granted for good behavior, we wander
the Upper East Side streets looking for decent coffee and
temporary comfort. I think of Ross, the healer, who told
me about spiritual initiation—the event that comes, shakes
up the personality and forces it to expand, to release into
a larger identity. I think, If only Sam could go away, into
a cave somewhere, with the Dalai Lama monitoring his
progress . . . *if only* . . .

Hanging out with Sam in the psych ward becomes my most pressing social engagement. And this engagement offers comfort. Warmth, even. Here, with him, I don't have to pretend to be okay. And we have fun. On any given evening, Sam entertains a handful of friends from college who sit in his hospital room as if it were a dorm at their Ivy League alma mater, telling stories and jokes, trying to help Sam feel *normal*. It's like a *Friends* episode behind locked doors, a salon full of the smart, dry, overeducated creative youth of New York. Except that at 9 P.M. we all ring for the nurse to let us back out into the world, our lives—and we leave Sam behind. Only I can't leave him behind. Usually, once home, I call the ward's pay phone to tell him something I'd remembered or witnessed on the way home. One night I say, "There is healing. A meadow. Transformation. And it's not just you, we are all being transformed and made new."

Sam asks, "Even Michael Jackson?"

And I say, "Yes. Even him."

Meanwhile, I'm still writing. That January I debut my one-act play *Nathaniel's Coming Out Party* at Dixon Place, an experimental performance gallery/theater/salon that operates out of founder Ellie Covan's living room. What started in 1986 as a weekly salon for friends to hear their "works in progress" has become a staple of the downtown performance scene. By 1994 they're on the Bowery, and I book a gig. Ellie appears at the beginning of each performance event to personally welcome the audience to Dixon Place—aka her home—and afterward she sells refreshments (beer, wine, herbal tea, etc.). I've cast *Nathaniel* with friends from my assorted jobs—Rainn from Beauty and the

Feast, Melinda from the Princeton Review, Rachel from DTW, and new friends Ben and Antoinette. I act in this play, too. We've been rehearsing in the director's apartment in Brooklyn Heights four days a week to prepare for the one-night-only showing, which is a great success. We are invited to bring the piece to the downtown storefront theater Todo Con Nada later that spring for an extended run—a whole weekend.

Two months later, we revive *Nathaniel* under its new name, *Generation X in Love,* and produce it along with the original short play from the Naked Angels production, now a full year ago. I love my walk to the theater each evening and my nights with the cast at El Sombrero afterward. I taste my first margarita (and wind up on a table lip-synching to "I Will Survive"). Soon after that, Solo 5 is invited to the Cleveland Performance Art Festival, where I perform one of my last pieces of solo theater, monologues about Marilyn Monroe, the approaching millennium, mental illness, and my mom. (The m-word theme is intentional.) But solo work is less fun than it used to be. Now that I've had a taste of actual playwriting, I want more. Plus, I'm convinced that the light I've been seeing—not just around Sam, but now intermittently throughout the day—is ushering in a period of accelerated spiritual growth, or at least a new direction. I can't explain it, but I know something is coming.

Sam is released from Payne Whitney and then promptly readmitted at his own urging; he claims that he's a danger to himself. His parents step in and decide to move him somewhere that's set up for more long-term care. The new hospital is in White Plains, roughly half an hour north on the commuter train. Sam's move to the suburbs reduces my

ability to visit, as I barely have the money for my weekly subway expenditures, let alone trips to Westchester and back. I
cannot imagine my week without the every-other-day visit
to my friend in the psych ward, and so the new plan engen-
ders a bad new habit. It's pathological, I know, but I begin
sneaking onto the Metro North trains, hiding in the bathroom, so that I can see him without paying the round-trip
ticket fee. The deception is easy: I board the train without
buying a ticket and head straight for the bathroom. Once
the train starts moving, I stay in the bathroom—reading,
writing—until the end of the ride. It's smelly but worth it.
And usually I can spend the whole half hour hidden and
uninterupted. The way I see it, the train is going there
anyway, so I'm not really stealing. Except that I am, and it
sucks, and in the end makes me feel bad about myself and
smell even worse.

For a few weeks, at the new hospital upstate, we pretend
that progress is being made. We try to carry on our old
precocious banter from Payne Whitney. But fewer people
are visiting, and Sam doesn't seem to be having any breakthroughs; he isn't getting better. At least, it looks like he
isn't getting better. And now I'm the only one insisting
there is a "better" to get to. Sam and his family and friends
all say, "It's the brain. There's so much we don't know..."
as if mental illness is the final line in a badly told story, and
there's nothing else to come. Plus, the doctors keep changing their diagnosis, and in the end they claim they don't
know what to do to help him.

"What are you doing?" asks Grace when I tell her about
my stowaway trips to Westchester. She pushes me, "What do
you want from him?"

"Nothing," I say. "I want him to heal."

"But what do you want for yourself?"

I'm defensive but later, in therapy, I admit my reasons for being such a diligent and faithful friend might be questionable. Grace is right. I'm overidentified with Sam's struggle, imagining that it is also mine, as if we are merged in our plight and in our paths. Worse, I'm replacing actual relationships with unincarcerated, mentally healthy people (okay, boys) by spending so much time thinking about, talking to, visiting (or buying bottled water for) Sam. I want to kidnap him and take him to some remote rural place where angels and Tibetan monks can administer to his deeper crisis—but I need to focus on my own deeper crisis at the moment and release Sam to his family, to his parents, and to his girlfriend. "This is not the man," says Grace. "And anyway, it's a really dumb moment to discover you're in love with your hospitalized best friend." I start to visit less. And, sadly, with some resistance, I turn my attention homeward.

Which is good because day-to-day operations on West Ninth are in jeopardy. Matt the Vegan Virgo and I barely get along anymore, and in acts of passive-aggressive defiance, I have begun bringing dairy products home, placing them in our refrigerator, to tempt, corrupt, pollute, or otherwise annoy him. Matt says, "The apartment isn't big enough for the both of us." And I say, "Really? Because I'm five foot one. Who's taking up all the room?" Or maybe I don't really say that, but I think it.

In an act of unprecedented generosity, Matt offers me the lease. It seems that he has been wanting to move to Brooklyn. But a few months later, when we're both still miserable and sharing domestic quarters, he admits there's no way he's giving up a West Village 2BR for under $1,100. It is I who must move.

But I'm in luck. Again. The Canadian girl who let me use her bathtub during the Thompson Street days is planning an extended trip back home and needs a subletter. She wants to see whether she can make a living in Canadian industrials and television, both of which are experiencing a boom in the early nineties. She may indeed return to New York in a few months' time, but she is hoping to "break in" and stay. And if she stays in Toronto, with a lucrative career in Canadian film and television, I will inherit her apartment, a rent-controlled studio in the East Village for under $400. It is absolutely worth the risk.

In addition, I've recently discovered a New Age book that echoes everything I've been saying to Sam—radical healing, radical transformation. This book says that we're part of a wave of ascending souls. I don't know much about *The Book of Revelation* in 1994, or the *Left Behind* series, which had yet to be written, or any kind of apocalyptic lore or eschatology, but I'm drawn to the notion that I might be part of a wave of souls who are only visiting, on our way back home. Why get stuck in long-term housing when we're spiritual beings on a temporary guest pass?

....

27 First Avenue

I move to 27 First Avenue just after Mother's Day 1994. The apartment is on the top floor of a building called the Ezra Pound, a small walk-up at the Lower East Side/East Village border, with a lovely wooden sign over the graffiti-covered door. Below the dedication there is a smaller handwritten sign. It says, *Don't piss here.*

Welcome home.

On my first couple of nights, I get used to the space: the pullout futon (this time, with a frame!), the bathtub (which has a prominent place in the kitchen, where it also acts as both counter space and table), and the creaky floorboards painted purple. The bookshelf is a Gen X postmodern primer: everything from *You Can Heal Your Life* to *Girlfriend in a Coma* to *The New York Agent Book*. Reserving judgment, I decide to read it all.

Soon after moving in, I am approached by the super, who happens to be the ex-boyfriend of the Canadian girl, asking, "Can I have a word with you?" I invite him into the apartment and listen as he explains, "I don't want to freak you out or anything, but we've found a bunch of decapitated pigeons and crack vials on the roof."

"What do you mean, you don't want me to freak out?"

The super continues, "It seems like someone's getting fucked up and cutting the heads off birds. . . . I don't think it's anything to worry about. It's probably kids . . ."

Words like "crack vials" and "decapitated" send me into full freak-out mode. What is he talking about!? I leave hysterical messages for the Canadian girl and my mother and then I start compulsively smudging—holding a wand of burning sage in front of me, clearing the energy of the apartment. By nightfall there is more sage than at a sun dance. It would set off the fire alarms, if we had any. Everyone—except my mother—says I'm probably fine. But I don't like the word "probably." When the Canadian girl finally returns my calls, she doesn't see what the big deal is.

She thinks the birds must be connected to the transsexual prostitute downstairs, who is known to practice Santeria here and there. (Apparently this neighbor began the series of medical procedures years ago, could not afford to continue, and has been in a bad mood ever since. Certainly s/he scowls every time s/he sees me on the stairs.) Or, agreeing with her ex, the super, the girl says "It's probably kids." But none of this is exactly *comforting*. And now, more than ever, I can't sleep.

It is now June, a full year since the rape—and this is my first attempt at living alone. I have lived in six apartments (if you count the "staying with friends" phases both before and after Brooklyn Heights) since the rape, and really, I want some place to settle—but nothing is forthcoming. Except decapitation and potential ascension. And the now-familiar refrain, "time takes time." Sam is released from the hospital, and he goes back to his parents' house to recover. I don't visit. Instead, I throw myself into a theater project— how better to survive the letting go of a failed crush? And a failed recovery effort? And decapitated birds?

Girls, Girls Girls: All One-Acts, All the Time is the name of the showcase that Melinda and I coproduce, along with four other female playwrights. Melinda finds a theater, and she and I start collecting plays. We assemble a company of writers, a director, and a line producer. We raise money, hire a stage manager and a publicist, and collectively produce the evening for a one-week run. Each playwright is responsible for casting her own play and hiring a director. *Generation X in Love* is joined by plays from Neena Beber, Leslie Buxbaum, Heather McCutcheon, and the late Adrienne Shelly. After two or three weeks of rehearsal, we run for one glorious sold-out week, and then, as if on cue, I run out of money.

Assembling *Girls, Girls, Girls* I hadn't had much time to work, and May is sort of a slow time for both Dance Theater Workshop and the Princeton Review. I've been living hand to mouth since April, and now that the show's over, I'm broke. Officially broke. As my mom would say, "el broke-o." With my last twenty bucks in hand, I treat myself to a $4 breakfast at the little café downstairs from my new (okay, *her*) apartment. I have a bagel and a cappuccino and look around, remembering that I've always liked this place. It's ridiculously small but unpretentious, oddly homey, if one's home were on the Beat poetry scene. Impulsively, I ask the Irish guy running the place, "Do you need any help here?" and am relieved—if not overcome with outright joy at the thought of having to waitress again—when he says yes.

"When can you start?" he asks.

I say, "Tomorrow."

And he gives me a set of keys.

I have somehow landed in East Village paradise: rent for just $375 a month and now a four-day-a-week job that more than covers my basic expenses. Exhausted from the year of spiritual transformation, rape recovery, and mental illness, and oddly relieved that the show is over, I decide to let go of everything that has previously defined me. Friends, goals, maybe even the dream of a career in the theater . . . and Sam. This summer, I vow, I'm going to let life happen, trust the new, and open myself to change. I will make new friends for the new world that my New Age sources assure me is coming.

The days at First Street Café are filled with just what I've asked for. I meet and befriend Charlotte, an Irish waitress and photographer who becomes my ally against obnoxious customers. ("What's your soup of the day?" asks Annoying Pretentious Patron. "I don't fucking know," answers Charlotte in her gorgeous accent, wide-eyed and innocently foulmouthed.) I befriend an English screenwriter; an opera singer from Minneapolis; and an aspiring actress who wears full-length 1970s caftans in bold colors while babysitting her NYU teacher's kids. I meet assorted members of what I'm later told is "Irish mafia;" a Canadian med student who confesses to be the ex-lover of Jean-Michel Basquiat; Veronica, the evening waitress who has a fetish for Rollerblades; and Neil, the Jewish bodybuilding co-owner of the café, who charms me by kicking people out of the establishment on a regular basis. "Get out of my fucking restaurant" he says whenever a customer pisses him off. These new people delight me. And I'm a total anomaly to them—a twenty-five-year-old virgin rape survivor performance artist slash aspiring playwright from the Midwest. I work four days a week at the café, starting at 7:30 A.M., when I raise the cranky metal gate and open the cranky old doors. We serve breakfast and lunch—anything you can make in a microwave and toaster oven (eggs courtesy of the milk steamer in the cappuccino machine). I stay until 4 P.M. when Veronica takes over. In addition to the joy of new companions, there is also the joy of a diet comprised entirely of bagels, coffee, and ice cream. I'm drinking something like five cups of coffee a day. Which might explain why I'm still not sleeping.

I stay up most nights, eating ice cream and trying not to be afraid. Every noise is an intruder, every creak in the floorboards an incipient rapist (or a "kid" on the roof killing birds). When I make my nightly Ben & Jerry's run, I'm aware that I'm substituting sugar and dairy for mothering, but I don't know how to get mothering, and I do know how to get a pint of cookie dough brownie fro-yo at Roger's, the twenty-four-hour deli across the street.

I start a meditation practice, my first, after reading Stephen Levine's *A Gradual Awakening*. Levine suggests that even ten minutes a day can make a difference. And so for ten minutes every morning before work, I sit cross-legged on the floor, close my eyes, and watch "the breath." The result? I have never felt angrier. I'm angry every day and restless every night as I wander up and down Avenue A wondering how anyone finds the place where they belong. Loneliness is a constant. Terror intermittent. Pain familiar. Bitterness is starting to surface. Maybe meditation has created a base, a calm in which these really horrifying feelings can (finally) come to light. But it's a drag. I snap at customers in the café, resenting that they're being served while I have to run around fetching things and cleaning up after them. Sometimes I remind them (and myself) that I was once on the honor roll at an Ivy League institution. (No one cares.) I yell at my mom when she calls long-distance. I break up with friends. I need help—and therapy isn't hitting it. The insomnia and anger and ice cream consumption are all building, and the results aren't good.

Enter Penney Leyshon, a miraculous spiritual healer who lives and works on the Upper West Side. As soon as I meet her, I know that Penney can help me. It's her gaze, which sees everything, and her quiet, calm, no-bullshit way of getting to the heart of matters. I rattle on, telling her about the Ascension, of which I'm part, and how I've been witnessing light streaming out of my friend Sam's skull in the mental hospital. I tell her how I've recently quit the theater and broken up with friends and put my things in storage in anticipation of my true calling. I tell her I'm writing letters to angels and reading books about spiritual transformation. I ask, "Am I going to be a healer, too?" And then, at the end of this long monologue about my material situation and spiritual dilemma, I add, "And I was raped a year ago, but I'm over that." Penney's eyebrows lift as she smiles ever so slightly, "You're over that? Really?"

Penney starts working, moving her hands gently over my body, barely touching me, as she shifts the energy and patterns. She speaks as her hands pull and then shake things off, reporting what she sees and what I need to let go of. It's as if she has access to my deepest core and can recognize what I am made of. It is soothing to be seen like this, but also, as the poet Rilke says of every angel, terrifying. Penney insists that this Ascension fetish is "ego," my psyche's way of trying to control and "act like a bigshot." She says, "You're so afraid to be in your body," suggesting that the real terror isn't about work or money or love but about being who I really am, embodied, which includes experiencing and processing the feelings from the rape. When I tell her I see light, she's unimpressed: "In the past, they killed you. Just for speaking up, for being who you are. You've been beheaded...your tongue's been cut out... you need to know that you can be safe, here, in your body, in this lifetime. You can bring your whole self *here*." Seeing lights flashing, she says, like other "New Age bullshit," is a distraction. "When people are healed here," she says, "they are ascended."

Penney says, "You're not over that rape yet. You don't have to be okay about it." Later, in subsequent sessions, she will say, "It's not okay, what that man did to you," and urge me to push her away, in the middle of the session, to give my body the release of pushing back instead of playing dead. She will say, "I want you to learn that someone can be close to you without being inside of you." But today, on this first visit, we start with basics. She tells me that my transformation, which, yes, is spiritual in nature, won't be full of rainbows and crystals—and might not be comfortable. Like any decent therapeutic process, it will take time. "It's not just you," she says, "the whole world is cleansing now. We're all cleansing . . . this is the time for it. Sometimes it feels like all we do is cleanse—like we can't get back to our lives until all of the garbage gets healed, comes up, and is released." But what else are we to do? If you don't release the garbage, heal the wounds, make yourself whole again, what good can you bring about in the world? What hope can you inspire? Penney asks if I will commit to my own healing, and I say yes.

I see Penney intermittently during those first few years. Not every week. Not even every month. But every few weeks or so, when we both feel it's right. I save money in between sessions in order to keep them going. Later I will barter services—writing, mostly—in order to keep seeing her and benefiting from her miraculous work. And still later, she will become a trusted, beloved friend and adviser, at times like a family member. Penney is able to name things for me, to pinpoint them and catalyze the internal (and eventually external) shifts that have eluded me in traditional talk therapy. She sees past the words, past the precocious smarty-pants language, into some deeper part of what I can only call soul. And it's raw. Sometimes ugly. But I agree with her about the necessity of plunging the depths, going down in order to come back up, exposing every fear and piece of unrecognized darkness to the light.

The summer isn't all caffeine and healing. By July, with the money I've saved through living cheaply and eating all my meals at the café, I decide to take a vacation. I've heard about a monumental astral occasion through my various New Age reading and Ravi Singh, the East Village Kundalini yoga guru—a comet, Shoemaker-Levy 9, is due to hit Jupiter (roughly, I note, the week of Henry David Thoreau's birthday, but that's significant only to me), and this is meant to impact the spiritual evolution of the planet in some way connected to the Ascension, though I don't particularly remember how. It seems like the ideal time to visit the City of Angels, Los Angeles.

I don't have credit cards and have never bought an airline ticket on my own. Waitresses without Visa cards depend on cash, so I follow a pink flyer in the café to a makeshift start-up company that sells standby vouchers from airlines you wouldn't want to travel on in the first place. Their flyer says, "If you can find a better deal, start your own damn airline." The guy who sells me the voucher promises a "95 percent success rate" so long as I'm willing to do the trial-and-error thing and go to the airport a few days in a row to see when I might get on a flight. What no one realizes is that this comet is hitting Jupiter the same week as the World Cup finals are hitting L.A. The airport is a circus, a Grateful Dead show packed with overzealous Brazilian soccer fans. Nobody is getting on any plane to

Los Angeles without a real ticket anytime soon. I call my excellent friend Ben and complain, "The Universe doesn't want me to go to L.A." He says, "I don't buy it. Use your will."

Determined, I look around the airport thinking, *How does one do that*? Isn't the point of spiritual growth to overcome the will? And now, it seems I need to activate mine? How do I use my will? I strike up a conversation with a cute guy I've had my eye on during these last two days of JFK comings-and-goings. He too has a standby voucher; he too has had his travel plans thwarted. I ask, "What are you doing about this situation?" Dan, a tall film geek who lives in Santa Monica, is relieved to have someone to talk to. We hatch a crazy plan. After stowing our bags in a locker in the airport and heading into Manhattan for Indian food, we call the airline and transfer our L.A. standby vouchers to San Francisco. The San Francisco flight leaves at 5 A.M. the following morning, so we spend a night—as if on a date—in lower Manhattan until the bars close and the sun rises and we head to the A train and the airport. We use our standby vouchers to fly to northern California, seated together on the plane, traveling as a couple. We arrive in San Francisco with hours to kill before the bus leaves, and so we spend a day shooting pictures in Haight-Ashbury. Then we take the Greyhound down the 101 to L.A. In his description this sounds easy and also like a good adventure. In real life, the bus takes eleven hours, and we stop getting along somewhere south of San Jose. I call Grace at 4 A.M. imploring her to come get me because I can't crash on Dan's floor. (He has a girlfriend.)

I spend a confusing week on Grace's pullout futon. She's wanted to see me for months, but I don't think she is prepared for the full-on New Age immersion. I can't shut up about the comet, yoga, and the dawn of an age in which all of us will be transformed and made new. I am a massive pain in the ass. Grace has recently gotten laid off and survived a visit from her parents, who kept demanding to know what she was doing with her life, so she's not much in the mood for white light, *A Course in Miracles,* or my endless talk of a kind of "party like it's 1999" spiritual redemption. The way she's feeling lately, she says, her ethos is: Plan for the worst, and be pleasantly surprised. I argue the exact opposite: *Why not anticipate the best? Why not imagine that you can have what you want? And that the Universe will support your deepest desires?*

We part on uncertain terms.

Back in New York, the café has lost its charm, and I feel trapped. What did I say in L.A. again? The Universe will support my deepest desires? I'm having a hard time remembering that. But one afternoon I run into the artistic director of a small theater who asks whether I have any full-length plays for his company. Lying, I say yes. And that week, I start my first.

Wonderland is about a search for spiritual redemption and healing in Hollywood. I will write and rewrite this play over the next two and a half years—and it will eventually earn me entrance into Juilliard and a career as a real playwright. But in August 1994 I'm not thinking of any of that. I'm just doing my thing day by day, wondering where it's all going and why the Wave that is "coming for me" is taking so long to arrive.

By early September the Canadian girl comes home, and I haven't disappeared or ascended. I need to find a place to live. Again. She suggests that we share the studio (and

her rent) until I find something, but at this point I just
can't see sharing a studio apartment with anyone. I don't
sleep through the night, and I seem to need a lot of privacy. Plus, the bathtub is in the kitchen, so what are we
talking about? I start looking at shares: Clinton Street,
Norfolk Street, Washington Street in Brooklyn. Nothing is right. Nothing is what I want. And nothing is cheap.

Penney says to take the next thing that looks safe and not
to worry about outcomes. She says, "Things are going to
change for you so many times over the coming years, I don't
get that you're staying put anywhere for very long." I look
at apartments, including one on the block, owned by a café
patron—the rent is more than I could even begin to conceive
of. I have yet to pay more than $550, and I have yet to earn
more than $10 an hour. How does anyone aspire to $1,100?
These are still the days of inexpensive studios downtown,
deals. But the days are starting to shorten, and as the Dylan
song goes, "the times they are a-changin'."

One afternoon, at the end of my shift, I confess my troubles to the girls I work with. By the end of my impassioned
monologue about how awful everything is, I am in tears. I
feel out of control and don't know what to do to help myself,
how to get from the picture where I'm obscure and homeless
to the picture where I'm happy and settled, employed and
housed. There is a missing link, I explain, between the idea
of what I want—a clean and beautiful apartment in lower
Manhattan with a bathtub and a closet—and the human steps
necessary to manifest that desire. Veronica, the Rollerblad-
ing beauty who works the night shift, is clear-eyed about the
whole thing. She says I need a boyfriend. But more important, she invites me to stay with her—for free—for a month.

It seems Veronica lives in an apartment that her parents own uptown, and she doesn't pay rent. No one has seen this apartment; we just know it's not in the neighborhood. Veronica says her parents, who don't even *live* in New York, aren't due back in town for another month or two, and I am "totally welcome to crash."

"Come on," she says. "Come back to my place. Stay until you have a plan."

Nodding—grateful and a little desperate—I say yes.

....

Trump Plaza, 167 East 61st Street

"Wait—you live here?" I ask, puzzled when I get out of the cab.

She shrugs.

Veronica's parents' apartment is on the twenty-first floor of one of the Trump high-rises—on the Upper East Side, a few blocks north of Bloomingdale's—with a view of Central Park. The parents themselves live in Pennsylvania and use this place as a "pied-à-terre."

"How come you didn't say anything?"

She shrugs again and leads me through the front door, past the doormen who seem amused by us both. I move in with just an army duffel—having left my boxes stacked in a corner at the Ezra Pound. The doormen are confused by me—my torn leather jacket, coffee-stained sandals, and big army duffel—even more so once I start meditating on the roof. But I take to Trump Plaza like Eloise to that other Plaza the Trumps own and immediately my sleep improves, my skin improves—insomnia is just another word for economic disparity. I'm sure that the tenants of this building receive special vitamin-enhanced filtered air along with a respite from the noise of the city below. Was this the trouble all along? I just needed a luxury high-rise and central air?

I take the Second Avenue bus to work the next day to discover I have been fired. ("We feel that you're more invested in your creative work anyway" and "Maybe the service industry just isn't for you.") Similarly, the Canadian girl demands that I remove my stash of boxes from her apartment. Why would I even imagine that it's her responsibility to keep them? I'm no longer paying her rent. Too embarrassed to ask Rainn and Holly—again—I hire another Man with Van from a sign in a local coffee shop and put my things into storage.

Ah, storage. I don't know much about storage in 1994—even the word sounds scary. Within a few years, I will know more than I ever wanted to. But in this virgin storage moment, I pick a space from the classifieds in the back of the *Village Voice,* one that offers a first-month incentive. For roughly $30 (plus The Man with Van) I stash my boxes, the mirror, and my lone piece of furniture (the dresser from Furniture Bob. Anything vaguely resembling a milk crate had been jettisoned after Ninth Street), into the storage space, where I no longer have to think about them or their safety.

While apartment hunting and now job hunting, I work on *Wonderland* and try to scare up more mailings and receptionist shifts at DTW. As I develop the play, the week in Los Angeles comes rushing back—the comet hitting Jupiter, the chaos of travel, my New Age fixation on "the light," the

strangers I befriended through yoga and meditation and
Marianne Williamson lectures, and my own confused and
conflated longings for spiritual redemption, Hollywood
fame and fortune, and an actual life as an artist. And then
the fight with Grace. And how I judged her, but later, back
in New York, understood what she was dealing with and
how she might feel. How can I urge someone to work from
vision and then lose all perspective when the vision needed
is my own?

So I write the play. In *Wonderland*, Mia, an aspiring performance artist, goes to L.A. to develop a sitcom about herself, and the show turns into what I can only now call "reality
TV." Once there, she meets all sorts of pop culture icons,
including Isaac the Bartender from *The Love Boat*, Bill Cosby,
Chrissy Snow, Marcia Brady, three black drag queens, an
eleven-year-old child, and Jesus Christ. Jesus, or at least my
irreverent *Course in Miracles*—inspired revisionist Jesus, is also
in L.A. developing a show. He wants to spread light and
the "good news" through television. "Fame in America in
the nineties is just a really different thing," he tells us. By
November I have a draft.

And also, by November, the next place to live.

....

274 West 19th Street

I answer an ad from the bulletin board at DTW one afternoon after a weekend-receptionist shift. The ad lists two
rooms in a rent-controlled 3BR apartment just across
the street. I rent the smaller room and Wes, an actor and
dancer recently back from a European tour of *42nd Street*,

rents the medium-sized room. In the largest room, by far twice the size of both mine and Wes's, lives Greg, an aspiring director. Coincidentally (although I don't believe in coincidence anymore), Greg and Wes went to high school together at the illustrious School of Performing Arts, aka the *Fame* school, and they used to work at Häagen-Dazs together. We don't talk about that part too often. We make a funny trio: Two boys (one gay and one straight), two cats (both neutered), and me.

Right away, Wes and I fall in love. In a matter of days, he becomes my platonic soul mate, big brother, and life coach. We stay up nights talking about love, life, The Theater, and our souls—all the stuff we want to create and all the love we want to express. Pretty soon, we are planning a road trip, Thanksgiving in the Berkshires. Wes's family lives near my expat New York friends, who have turned macrobiotic. (Macrobiotic: It means "big life" and involves a lot of brown rice.) We leave New York, stop in New Haven to flirt with Yalies, and then, arrive at the Kushi Institute (KI), a macrobiotic teaching facility and commune outside Becket, Massachusetts. This is where I first lay eyes on Noah Stern.

Noah is the twenty-one-year-old head chef at the KI, and at this particular moment he is dating a friend of mine. One night, while everyone else has gone in search of something neither of us cares about, we borrow a car and drive to the nearby yoga retreat, where we sneak into the hot tubs. There are separate tubs for men and women so I do not see his naked body, but already I am thinking about it. Later, as we're driving home through the snow, talking like old friends, Noah says, "Whenever I get too lost in my own head, I remember the Infinite Universe . . . and it's like, I can do anything." I stop listening at "the Infinite Universe" and melt, thinking, "Someday this will be an amazing man."

And then I forget all about him. Entirely. After all, he's dating my friend. And I'm still in love with Sam in the loopy farm. Right?

When Wes and I get back to New York, my primary focus is financial. I've had the luxury of working on *Wonderland* for the last two months, but now I can't even think about creative goals because I can barely pay my bills. My rent is $525 a month, and I need a job to supplement my insufficient DTW income.

At this point, I've worked solely in arts administration and restaurants. But now, feeling desperate, I pursue office work. My first day at the temp agency, I am told (as with the first time I tried this years ago) that, yes, I must purchase and wear panty hose and also comb my hair. ("You look a little . . . arty. Like, unkempt," says the lady with the heavy accent. She looks like Joan Cusack in *Working Girl* but I'm too broke to argue.) Preparing to temp is like life with my mother all over again. Outfits are required. Hair must be neat, no inkstains on nails, a suit if I can stomach it (or afford to buy one!). But still, sitting at a computer terminal in panty hose—drinking coffee no less—beats running my ass around a busy restaurant. I buy the panty hose: black with seams up the back, like in a 1940s movie. I'm determined to succeed in the corporate temp world. And succeed I do. Each job asks to rehire me. What I lack in personal hygiene, I make up for in vocabulary. I even learn to work the fax machine.

I temp for a brief two months until a friend of a friend offers me a job working for her mother's foundation, where I catalog and assemble the incoming grant applications for an Italian fellowship. While working for this foundation, I am discovered by two pretty twenty-somethings with Yale degrees helming a new nonprofit called Libraries for the Future (LFF). The visionary director of this organization has founded LFF with the goal of catalyzing a wave of support for public libraries, separate from the American Library Association, which is composed solely of librarians. She imagines a citizens' movement. The libraries have been hit by severe cuts in funding and, as LFF sees it, their future is in mobilizing ordinary citizens to raise awareness and money locally, community to community. I learn that the public library is one of the great, true democratic structures—an organization where, by virtue of nothing else but applying for a card, anyone can share books and information and gain literacy skills, public health information, voting and citizenry support, and now, public access to the (very new in 1995) Information Superhighway, or Internet.

When my job at the foundation ends, I am literally scooped up by LFF, where the twenty-somethings create a job specifically for me: advocacy assistant. As advocacy assistant (I feel like a superhero!), I seek ordinary people who have identified themselves as defenders of their local library, stepping up to support or fund-raise. I interview these people, "amplify" their stories, and connect them with other advocates through an Internet Listserv/discussion group on libraries, which I moderate. This is the first "real" job—a salary, my own desk and computer console, an e-mail account—that I have ever held. Trading one acronym for another, I quit DTW to join the team at LFF. When I excel at finding and linking the library advocates, they promote me and soon "assistant" has turned into "coordinator." This brings benefits, plus new responsibilities and new clothes. While I don't have to cover my bare legs (except in winter, and that's for warmth), I also can't sustain the arts organization thrift shop dress and torn leather jacket ensembles I'm used to wearing. I go for something in between—crunchy save-the-world loose-fitting skirts and T-shirts in more shades of green and brown than I ever imagined possible.

At twenty-six, after six years of pursuing a life in the arts, public libraries feel immediate and important. I think, Maybe this is how I'll be a healer. Through helping to mobilize a citizens' movement. Through reaching and connecting with all of these strangers and then helping them help themselves! Maybe all those years in the theater were training me to have an effect somewhere else. *Maybe*—and I don't say this, but now looking back, it's what I was thinking—*this will be my home.* I tell Heidi, "I'm going to be a healer through the public library system," and she says, "My God, you belong in the theater. You're so dramatic."

My life settles into an unexpected—and unexpectedly stable—groove. Health insurance and taxicabs. Computer literacy and—still rare in 1995—the Internet! There are weekend parties and 6 P.M. cocktail hours at Grand Central Station with my fellow library-loving coworkers, conferences and meetings where I learn about the nonprofit sector, and words like "collaborative" and "coalition," "synergize" and "catalyst." My New Age and theater vocabularies fit, strangely, with the Yale- and Harvard-educated social action crew (We, too, are seeking to unify, synergize, catalyze, and create!). I feel like an idiot savant in discussions and meetings. All of which helps engender the belief that maybe, maybe this is where I belong, and maybe, maybe these activists will be my family.

But the Infinite Universe has other plans for me. And they don't include job stability or Chelsea.

One night I return home from an LFF think-tank "retreat" to find that we three roommates have been slapped with an eviction notice. It's big and ugly and it says, *You have thirty days to vacate.* I discover that, unbeknownst to Wes and me, Greg has been in debt to the landlord during our entire tenure in this apartment. Furthermore, it seems, our rent has been applied to Greg's debt each and every month—increasing the arrears on the apartment and incurring fees. And my name and Wes's name are not recognized as leaseholders. We confront Greg, but he is as confused about the whole thing as we are. "This has to be wrong," he says—but then admits, yes, he knew the apartment was in arrears. And, yes, he knew the exact amount of the debt when we moved in.

Wes and I are furious. Why didn't he tell us? How could he *not* tell us! Greg doesn't see it that way. It's news to him that our rent checks were going toward the arrears and not to current rent. It's news to him that we're not leaseholders. *But why is this news? Why didn't he know? Why didn't he tell us he was this far in?*

We offer to take over the lease—without him—and start again. But the management company that runs our building won't hear of it. It seems that this apartment has been handed down, friend to friend, on one lease for so long that it's way beneath market value. It's not "rent controlled," as I was led to believe, but rather a lease that has never been forced to change hands or "turn over." The three of us are still paying a base rate that the original leaseholders negotiated, probably a decade ago. The landlords are pissed. They want a fair market price. And since we can't pay it, we have to go. We consult Jane, an old tenants-rights advocate who lives in our building. Jane says, unless we want to go to housing court, we have no recourse. The bottom line is: Greg is in debt to the landlord. Greg is on the lease. We are not on the lease. The apartment is not ours.

Resentfully, I start looking at shares in the evenings and on weekends. But before I can make too much progress, Wes hits me up with a plan. He has found a place in Brooklyn—the entire second floor of a building for $1,050 a month. And even though he wants to live alone, and I want to stay in Manhattan, the space and the price are both right. Soon we are on our way.

. . . .

131 Fifth Avenue, Brooklyn

I hate Park Slope. As Bess, the precocious NYU student, says in my play *Hunting and Gathering,* "Park Slope is this really funny part of Brooklyn where everyone pretends they live in Woodstock, only they don't. . . . It's basically a white liberal ghetto for Wesleyan grads with Asian babies. Honestly, I'm over the entire borough. It takes way too long to set anywhere, and you have to act like you care about communal food." (An homage to the infamous Food Co-op.) Yes,

I am aware of the gracious brownstones with their stained-glass windows, the pretty tree-lined streets, stoop sales, and the joys of Prospect Park. But every time I live here, I feel trapped.

In 1995 Fifth Avenue is not yet home to the shiny happy Wesleyan grads—it's still rough. Where there are now sushi fusion joints and nouveau bistros and eclectic boutiques, there used to be 99 Cent Stores and a Mr. Eggroll franchise. Wes says, the week we look at the new apartment, "In a few years, all this will gentrify. It'll be bigger than Seventh Ave." Stupid me, I'm not a believer. "You just want me to move in with you," I say, wrinkling my nose like a spoiled teenager. Years later, I'll call him up from the Asian-fusion-sake-espresso bar on our old block to admit, "You were right."

Our apartment covers the entire second floor of a small three-story brownstone, above a Blimpie and across from the big Key Food supermarket. It's enormous. We each have two private rooms of our own, bedrooms and offices, in addition to an ample-sized living room, eat-in kitchen, hallway, and a bathroom with tub (which Wes will paint midnight blue). Also, it's unfurnished. This is the very first time that I will have (at least partial) decorating carte blanche. Wes has definite ideas about it—I mean, this is a gay Virgo with carpentry skills and aesthetic standards, for goodness' sake! But I am allowed to do what I like with both of my two rooms. (What I like is to ask his advice.)

We buy futons together at the futon store and rugs and carpet samples at the ABC outlet, and then he leaves me to my own devices and imagination. After living in bedrooms the size of walk-in closets, this freedom to create is mind-boggling. I barely know where to start. I find an upholstered armchair at a thrift shop in Prospect Heights, a desk on the street in Chelsea, a desk chair on the street in Park Slope—you see, back in the nineties, before the Bed Bug Crisis, one could furnish entire apartments through Dumpster diving. Or, really, without ever involving an actual Dumpster, by patrolling certain affluent neighborhoods on garbage night to see what treasures one's neighbors had left out in the street for recycling. I take pride in finding art, furniture, and, at times, clothing in this magpie manner. It is a delight. "Where'd you get that great skirt/chair/television set?" "Oh, I found it on the street!" A badge of honor.

I try to explain to Wes, "This is what I love about thrift shopping . . . the total chance of the thing, the fact that you're always at the mercy of fate."

"This is what I love about Barney's," he counters, "the fact that you're not." And again, as when we moved to Nineteenth Street, there are long walks and meals and nights spent talking. But despite our camaraderie the neighborhood is lonely. I hate commuting to Midtown (the B train is my new best friend) and walking home from the subway, alone, late at night. Living half an hour away on the train— and working full time—changes my habits. I have less time for the kind of friendships I've previously known. No more sitting in coffee shops, wandering Tompkins Square, wasting the afternoon waiting for a four o'clock waitressing shift—or, rolling out of bed for a seven-thirty waitressing shift. No more nights watching dance concerts (no more DTW—so no more free tickets!). And no late rehearsals and postshow bonding with other "theater people." I have to be up and out the door too early for any of that, and public library advocacy leaves me with little energy for theater. I tell myself I'm living a "real" life now. I start hanging out more with my new coworkers, going for drinks in Grand Central and dinners uptown.

"You're never here," Wes points out. "Despite all your talk of wanting a home, you're never *in* the one that we have." And then comes the piece of advice that I will take with me, remember, and repeat over all the years to come. He says, "The only way to *have* a home is to *make* a home. Spend time in it. Invest your energy. Be here." I'm speechless. I know that he's right. But I can't sit still. I'm twenty-six years old, none of my friends live in the Slope or the Heights or anywhere I can walk to—Anya has long since moved on—I'm used to the East Village, which moves differently and at different hours. And I don't want to be here.

Let us be fair. There is nothing wrong with Park Slope. When I lived on Bergen Street with Anya during those few months in 1991, I pretended it was Vermont. But for whatever reason, right now, "pretend" isn't working. Coming home, and especially the late-night walk from the subway to our apartment, I feel cut off and isolated. And he's right— as I spend my days at work and my nights with friends, our place on Fifth Avenue feels more like his and less like mine. This becomes even more poignant when he loses his job, turns thirty, and starts hibernating. It feels like something sacred and mysterious is occurring within his room and office, behind closed doors—and sometimes like I'm in the way. We still have our share of adventures, but he's changing. And so am I.

At the end of August, after living in the apartment for roughly three weeks, Wes goes on a trip, and I lose my virginity to a Library Advocate I've met through my Internet

discussion group. Really, I have no idea how it happens—
I'm not even particularly attracted to him until we kiss.
In fact, I have a crush on someone else. But the Library
Advocate is my only Park Slope friend. And one night,
after walking me home, he plants the most exotic and kind
of amazing kiss on my previously unkissed lips, and without
thinking about it too much, I invite him upstairs where
our clothes come off and we initiate my new futon. Actual
intercourse sex is a revelation. I don't tell him about the
rape; I don't tell him that I'm a virgin; none of it feels
particularly relevant. My narrative, the overly digested
ironic story I've gotten used to telling about myself, melts
away and something else, something unexpectedly joyous,
transpires. I feel free.

Afterward, everything is different. The Advocate, who I
now believe I am in love with, says, "I don't believe in casual
sex. I think we should either try to have something or, you
know, not . . ." Flushed, I say, "Let's have something." But
the next morning, and in the days after, he changes his
tune. He no longer wants to "have something." He kind
of wants me to go away. I don't go away. Like the Liz Phair
song I listen to obsessively, *I want a boyfriend*. The Library
Advocate is bisexual, so maybe he wants a boyfriend, too.
One thing he does not want is me. I'm devastated and write
sad, awful poetry about it.

A month later, my mother visits. She insists on staying
in Manhattan, at a Midtown hotel, and I insist on staying in
my own apartment, making dates with her instead of sharing a room. This is a new boundary. We have dinner on
the Upper West Side. She meets Penney for a healing session, which is very interesting to me—it means she's trying.
And she agrees to come see my apartment in Brooklyn,

which means she's really trying. She has not been to any of my abodes since Thompson Street, and I'm excited to show her where I've been living, and with whom. We plan a brunch.

"She's going to ask what you do for a living," I warn Wes, who's still unemployed.

"I'll tell her the truth. I take care of the daughter she fucked up."

He doesn't. And despite my mom's taxicab trauma ("Brooke? The driver dropped me off some place called Sunset Park. Is that near where you live? I just kept telling him that it's across from the big Key Food"), we have a pleasant meal at one of those little Park Slope brunch places that seduces me into thinking I could like the neighborhood. Then she goes back to Detroit. And as always, after seeing her, I crash. There are days of confusion and uncertainty. Guilt for wanting my freedom. And more guilt for having gotten it.

Work is no refuge. These days, LFF feels more like an impotent think tank than an actual citizens' movement. The cute twenty-something wunderkind running LFF has gotten accepted into a prestigious graduate program in public policy and has been replaced by an older, highly experienced, Blue Blood Bostonian Do-Gooder. The Do-Gooder revamps our "organizational image" and hires extra managerial staff (Angela, the office manager, points out that we're an office of managers without any worker bees) and "strategic" consultants. I am often stuck doing unpaid overtime, finishing proposals, writing up advocates' stories, completing "best practice" briefs, and locating "key" new contacts who my boss may have spoken to on a bus somewhere without explaining to them why she wanted to add them to our growing network. Truthfully, I love the work. What I do not love is the fact

that I'm in the office after hours most nights a week, checking the Listserv and e-mails from home and basically living my job without being fairly compensated or even really
respected. I resent that in the absence of paid overtime, I
can't take "comp hours." I resent that they resent that I ask.
I'm working my ass off, and I can't remember why. After the
twenty-somethings go, I'm left without friends in the office,
or allies; I feel underappreciated and put-upon. Welcome
to the full-time workforce. Welcome to the nonprofit sector
where, one foundation at a time, we're changing the world
and underpaying our employees.

One Friday night, well past midnight, as I'm leaving
a dance party at St. Patrick's Youth Center on Mulberry
Street, some friends and I hit the ATM so I can take out
$40, enough for a cab back to Park Slope. I'm shocked
to discover that my bank account is empty—completely
empty—and now, with the unavailable-funds notice, in
arrears. The bank assesses a fee for attempting to take
money out when there is no money, even on payday when
direct deposit has assured me that money should be there.
I can't understand the mistake—direct deposit has been
paying me this way since I got on payroll four months ago.
What has happened? And, more saliently, how will I get
home tonight? And what will I eat tomorrow? A friend
lends me $20 to get through the weekend, and I take the
subway home, where I spend the next forty-eight hours
eating spaghetti and trying not to leave the house.

On Monday, I demand to know what has happened. My
boss explains that they had a delay in meeting payroll and
thus didn't pay anyone. The other employees knew, since
they were in the meeting at which such a plan was discussed.
But no one told me. No one called, and no one e-mailed.

Furious, I explain that if she'd given me some kind of advance warning, I could have made other plans. But there was no warning, and thus no time to plan. Just a bank fee and a borrowed twenty. And there's still no money in my account.

"Are you going to lend me a hundred dollars? No?" I demand. "Because really, without that, I'm fucked."

She doesn't like being yelled at. She sends me back to my desk, outraged that I've dared to challenge her in such a manner. "You'll get paid eventually," she says, as if it's my fault for doubting. But what am I supposed to do in the meantime? I have no contingency plan, and I've sworn off Marilyn's already maxed-out credit cards. I walk back to my desk thinking, What am I doing? I came to New York to work in the theater. To be an artist. First an actress, then a performance artist, then a writer. And I took this job in order to have a paycheck. What I'm most offended by is the assumption that it's permissible to not communicate. Only a rich person expects his or her employees to wait on their salary or to "understand" and be patient when communication is withheld. I can't see straight. I can't even open my e-mail account without fury blinding me. And this is one of those moments that I both regret and will be forever proud of: I walk off the job. I'm Sally Field in *Norma Rae*, Peter Finch in *Network:* "I'm mad as hell, and I'm not going to take it anymore." And all this for one paycheck! I quietly walk out, telling Angela that I'll come back when some form of salary appears in my bank account.

I am practically giddy, high on adrenaline as I head to the East Village, thinking, I'm not a victim, I have options. Even if some of those options include doing something as utterly self-destructive and fucked up as walking off the job. I show up, flushed, at Charlotte's place on Clinton Street, and we spend the day painting our toenails blue and making plans for future abundance. We promise to buy things like curling irons and vibrators once we both start making money "from our art." Playing hooky feels great. But later that night, after a long talk with Wes, I agree to go back to work on Tuesday as if nothing has happened. I need this job.

I show up the next morning in my appropriate earth colors, ready to be a docile Library Advocate again, when I'm called into the executive director's office and given the boot.

"Clearly," she says, "you'd rather be doing something more creative. And thus, you're not giving us your best self"—as if to make the problem mine. She doesn't address the elephant in the room, which is the simple question, Why did you not tell me you weren't meeting payroll and provide some kind of contingency plan? Why was there no dialogue about something so integral to the very contract of a job? I work for you in order to get compensated. It is my responsibility to work, but yours to pay me for said work. Instead, I'm talked down to, as if I'm an unruly child that she's put up with long enough. And so that afternoon, after being humiliated and fired, I pack up my desk and leave for good. I come home to Wes, who's already on unemployment, and ask, "Now what?" By the end of the year, I've applied for unemployment benefits myself and started writing my first résumé. We spend a quiet holiday season at home in Park Slope. Wes rents *Gone with the Wind* from the public library because, in his words, he wants to start 1996 hearing Scarlett say, "Tomorrow is another day."

It is January 1996, and I feel that I'm at the bottom of a very tall well wondering, *What am I going to do to get out of here? Where is the light? And how do I change?*

Wes and I are now both unemployed and transforming at a rapid pace. We borrow movies from the public library and steal the Sunday *New York Times* Arts and Leisure section (and occasionally job ads) from the coffee shop on Seventh Avenue. We make huge pots of soup (or macaroni and cheese) and eat all of our meals at home. We take long walks around the perimeter of Prospect Park and wait for spring. At least, I do. I apply for jobs, and I get new headshot pictures taken, thinking, Maybe now is the time to recommit to being an actress. I start submitting the two plays I've written to small theaters, including New Georges, a company specializing in work by emerging women artists. And I get cast in an experimental theatrical reinterpretation of the Passion play (as Pilate's wife).

My spiritual practice has never been stronger, and I need my sessions with Penney more than ever. I read the Gospels and the book of Job and the Buddha. I practice exercises from *A Course in Miracles*. I light candles. I talk to psychics. I meditate. I ask something, anything, to start making sense and to carry me "home."

In February I go back to the Berkshires and attend a wedding at the Kushi Institute, the macrobiotic commune where I'd spent that lovely Thanksgiving. I am greeted by Noah Stern, who is no longer dating my friend. He is definitely available. Plus, he has these really sexy green-hazel eyes, a *Guide to Intentional Communities*, and an atlas in his room—not to mention dreams of future travel.

"We should hang out," he says.

I am more than happy to oblige.

Noah and I drive the hour and a half to Northampton, Massachusetts, for soy lattes, which are forbidden at the macrobiotic commune. I love the way he can't quite look at me but then, when he thinks I'm looking elsewhere, indulges—all the while clutching a molasses brownie in his hand like some talisman blessed by a holy person. I also love the way he talks about food—like someone who was raised macrobiotic but has the DNA of an Upper West Side New York Jew. Meaning, he knows all about nori seaweed and dairy-free tofu quiche but covets smoked salmon and bear claws. When we get back to the commune, Noah randomly offers to waterproof my snow boots, and I think, Why not? We go up to his room in the Kushi dorm, and I watch as he spreads mink oil all over the surfaces of the boots I picked up earlier that year on Second Avenue. Somewhere after the mink oil and before the dinner bell, we have our clothes off, thrown across his floor in strange patterns, and we are underneath his down comforter exploring the unknown territory of each other's bodies. We are in his room for hours. The sun sets; dinner comes and goes. He puts his clothes on to get food and brings a plate and chopsticks back upstairs. And then I have to take his clothes off all over again so I can see and touch him. There are freckles covering his beautiful shoulders, and I'm already in love. He is the second man that I've had sex with, or even seen naked for that matter, and the first to open my heart. I do not spend the night, but instead wind my way back down the hill, to sleep on the pullout couch at my friend's place. The next night, when I do sleep over, I run my fingers through Noah's hair as he sleeps, thinking, *May you be blessed. May you be happy. May you be healthy. May you be free from suffering.* Because already I like him that much.

I go back to New York a few days later. We have no real plans to keep in touch. After my debacle with the Library Advocate, I'm wary of expressing attachment or need. So I don't. And I'm amazed when Noah shows up on my door-step in Park Slope two weeks later, with all of his belongings in his red van—as he's leaving the Berkshires for a private cooking job in Virginia. We spend a weekend together and talk, very loosely, about driving across the country when his job in Virginia comes to an end.

Now, driving across the country has always been a partic-ular fantasy of mine, one that I've never had the wherewithal (or money or car) to pursue. But Noah has the van. And the atlas. And we're already crazy about each other. He is every-thing I have been yearning for—sweet, soulful, intuitive, brave, and really, really sexy. Noah is sexy in that "raised by hippies" way. He has no accumulated religious guilt about sex or the body, no fear of women (having been raised by a strong single mother), and no fear of me. Maybe all those friends who urged me to "get off the career path" two years ago were right. Maybe, just maybe, I think, what I seek is in the arms of this tall stranger with the sweet-smelling freck-led shoulders. Maybe if we leave New York in his van and head west, into the Unknown, like in a really good novel or *Easy Rider*—maybe everything will be made clear. Maybe this is what I have been waiting for.

. . . .

The Road Trip

We leave New York on April 15, just after mailing taxes. I have sublet my room(s) to an old friend of Wes's who will move out abruptly, leaving me with her unpaid phone bill—but I don't know this yet. I think everything is fine.

We load my futon and assorted clothes and books and cassette tapes into the van. He's had the backseats taken out so that we can unroll the futon and sleep back there. This will become relevant soon enough. But not yet. We spend the first night at his mother's house in western New Jersey, spooning on her couch, watching VH1. To the background of Katrina and the Waves' "Walking on Sunshine," Noah says, "I don't know what falling in love feels like, but I think I am . . . in it . . . with you," and we fall asleep in each other's arms. Noah holds on to my hips, all through the night, as if he will never let go. And I love it. I want him to hold on to me, just like this, forever.

The next day, we arrive in Pittsburgh, where Noah has a two-week cooking job. As part of the job, we have free housing and unlimited groceries from the local health food co-op. Safe and fed and loved, I start to write my second play, a one-act about Sam in the psychiatric hospital. Noah cooks two meals a day for his client, a bedridden diabetic with two broken legs and an overabundance of Noam Chomsky literature. And the rest of the time, we make love and explore Pittsburgh, a surprisingly brilliant city in which to have a hippie macrobiotic honeymoon. We visit museums, parks, and coffee shops, and every afternoon, while Noah cooks, I sit on the porch thinking *it's as if I am being rewired.* My circuitry is expanding through love, sex, and Noah's brilliant cuisine. In addition to the delicious hot breakfast cereal every morning (with currants, nuts, seeds, and oats), he cooks fragrant curries, orange-peel tempeh, lentil stew with basmati rice and corn, even vegan lasagna made with beet puree! (The colors alone are dazzling—the taste of it, divine.) Then, after the macrobiotic dinners, we

go in search of the other things he craves—corned beef sandwiches and French toast from the places we discover near the
waterfront. I crave only him.

In Pittsburgh I call my mom. "I'm on a road trip with a
boy," I say. "He's kind of my boyfriend. He's twenty-two."
She says, "I'm divorcing The Archduke." She says, "I want
to be happy again." And then, "If you get to New Orleans,
on your trip," she advises, "be sure to go to Antoine's and
have a beignet."

But my mother does not divorce The Archduke, and
Noah and I never make it to New Orleans. Both of our
routes will be haphazard. My mom will discharge her surly
and semiparalyzed husband to a nursing home—after
which her own health will start to disintegrate. And after
roughly five weeks of driving across the country (three
weeks in Pittsburgh, a few days with friends in Chicago,
then westward—through Oklahoma and north Texas sleeping in the van in church parking lots, a few days with Grace
and her new boyfriend in New Mexico, then hitting state
parks in Colorado, Utah, and Nevada), Noah and I will
arrive in San Francisco broke and smelly.

We spend our last $300 on a room in the Mission, in the
apartment of an Irish poet whose nom de plume is meant
to remind one of one of the cruder references for female
anatomy. At Noah's urging, we head to the Sierra Nevada
for an eleven-day silent Buddhist meditation retreat and
then, fully detached, return to the city to deal with our
dwindling funds. By "dwindling" I mean we've run out of
money. Entirely.

Noah says, "The Universe will take care of us." But it
doesn't. Or maybe it does, because I get a job as an office
manager at a new media firm in a neighborhood called the

China Basin. Noah gets a job, too—through the insanely
well-connected macrobiotic underground—as a private
chef for a family of rich vegans recovering from cancer in
Napa Valley. And then a whole lot of other things happen—
including a pregnancy scare, mystical instruction in the
Kabbalah, and a beautiful ride up the Pacific Coast to Portland and Seattle in a 1968 Volvo with a hot stranger whom I
meet through the rides board at Rainbow, the health food
store. But basically, by the end of August, Noah is living in
his van in a parking lot outside a doughnut shop in Santa
Cruz, and although I'm still ridiculously in love with him,
I need to move on. "Where I come from," I try to explain,
"people don't live in vans." Stubbornly, he claims he's "this
close to Enlightenment" and any form of work might distract him from his purpose. We have the same fight over
and over again—and over and over again, make love in the
van anyway—until finally I decide it's time to go home. If
only I could figure out where that *is*.

My Kabbalah teacher (and friend), a musician from
Brooklyn, tells me, "There is a doorway open for you
now." Why not step through the doorway? Stay in the west?
Change my life? "Old Brooke is dead," she warns. And I'm
tempted to stay. There is even a room available in Grace's
ex-boyfriend's house in Portland, Oregon. I could move
in, buy a used car, maybe get my massage therapy license in
the pursuit of some money-earning skill. But there is no
job I am qualified to do in Portland (or Fairfax, California, for that matter) at which I could earn more than $9 an
hour. And when I'm really honest, I have to admit I still
want to work in the New York theater. Even if I still won't
totally admit that to myself. I spend agonizing days on
the floor of Powell's bookstore reading whatever tracts on

"inner direction" that I can get my hands on until finally I buy an airline ticket at Dirt Cheap Travel. Back to New York City. I guess I've found some direction. Or at least the ability to take a stand.

I say good-bye to the state of California in a field outside San Luis Obispo during Labor Day weekend, promising that someday, if it's "in everyone's highest good," I'll return. Noah drives me to the airport in San Francisco, walking me all the way to the gate (something you could do before September 11). Neither one of us can stop crying. We don't want to let go. But what else can we do?

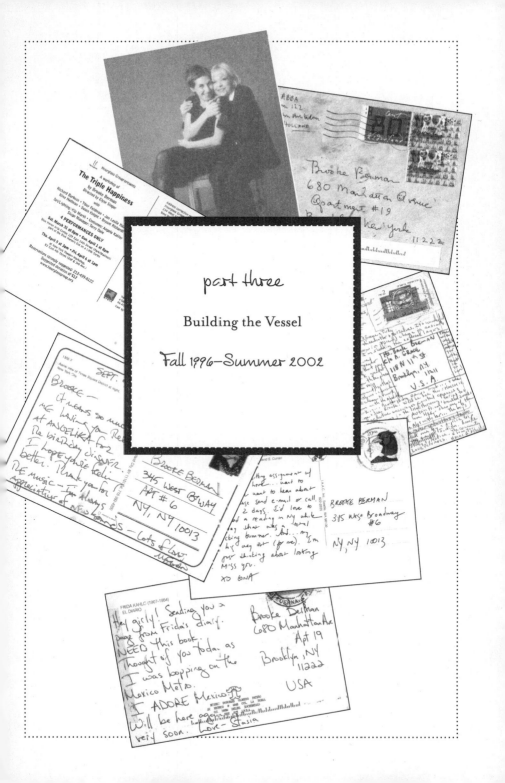

part three

Building the Vessel

Fall 1996–Summer 2002

160 Front Street, New York
Daigle Road, Putney, Vermont

In September, back in New York City, in debt to
both Sprint and Montgomery Ward (but we really
did need that video camera in Oklahoma), it is time to
reassess.

Getting "off the career path" has not improved my life.
Giving up dairy and eggs and caffeine has slightly improved
my life. The breathing exercises I learned from the Kabbalah teacher have definitely improved my life. Having a
boyfriend has made my life significantly richer but significantly more complicated—at times even hard. Working
in an office in San Francisco wasn't any better than any
job I've had anywhere else. And the Buddhist meditation
guru in the mountains bugged me. I left the retreat center
thinking, I want to go to L.A. and make movies.

When I first get back to town, I spend a month subletting
from Lee, a friend with a duplex loft on Front Street, just
off the South Street Seaport. She and her sister have been
sharing this apartment, which they've rented from their dog
groomer, who lives in New England. The dog groomer keeps
the lease in her name and visits once a month or so, while Lee
and her sister are the day-to-day tenants. The space is huge,
and the neighborhood sleepy. All business all day, all quiet
all night. This loft has long been my favorite of my friends'
apartments. Lee and I have spent many nights upstairs in
her room, watching TV and gossiping about boyfriends and

auditions, while planning the rest of our creative lives. We've even written together. But now Lee and her sister are moving on—Lee to L.A. and her sister to Maine. And so, during the packing and dismantling of the apartment, I sublet the downstairs bedroom; our friend Mia, who is just starting grad school, sublets the large living room; and the three of us help Lee say good-bye to her NYC life.

Noah is still in California, which he insists on calling "Cali" every time we speak, which is roughly three times a day. He has my futon, rescued from the van, at his mother's new place in the Central Valley, and he sleeps on it, in her living room, as he works out his next move. "If you come back to New York," I say, "we could date." He is unmoved. "Or if you get a job in California," I suggest, unable to use the nickname "Cali," "I could join you." Again, nothing. But despite his inability to make a plan, he sends me care packages full of butter-and-sugar-chocked nonmacrobiotic chocolate chip cookies and mix tapes and even a pink feather boa.

I don't know where to settle, how to pay for it, or what to do next. I want to be with Noah, but Noah isn't anywhere I could join him. (I don't want to live in his mother's living room; I've just gotten rid of my own mother, why would I get attached to someone else's?) I don't know if I want to stay in New York. But I don't know where else to go. And yet, I know I'm not quite ready for reentry. I need a plan. . . . And so when October comes, I take a bus to Vermont, where I've arranged a work-study exchange with my friend Flo Aeveia at her nonprofit, aptly named Soul Support Systems.

Flo Aeveia is another contact from the days of the postrape shamanic therapist. I have read her channeled books, spoken with her, received a "soul blueprint" reading from the

Nameless Ones, even arranged a visit (in November 1995, a welcome respite from the library job). This month in residence, staying at her house while working in the office, a work-study exchange that I have initiated, will be important. Although I'm just doing administrative work—transcribing and editing and helping with the Web site—in truth, I feel that I'm there to reconnect with myself and soul and to absorb whatever energy I can from the two hundred acres of Vermont wildlife and assisting angels. "Holographic living," Flo calls it. During the month in Vermont, I finish the new play and start a screenplay about my summer in San Francisco with Noah. *Shlomo Has Four Daddies* posits, post–pregnancy scare, what if Noah and I had had a baby? And what if—and this is years before Madonna's *The Next Best Thing*—what if I raised that baby with my gay best friend and his boyfriend in a house in Poughkeepsie? I ask the Infinite Universe for a vision, some clue as to my next step or direction, and one day, while sitting under a tree, just like Buddha did, I receive the following: *Eat meat. And apply to grad school.*

That night I eat chicken. And a few days later, I return to New York City just as Noah is returning from California. Once I set up my "B job"—the jobs we take to earn money while pursuing our real work—and a few temporary structures, I can research and apply to graduate school. But first, a free sublet.

....

636 Washington Street

I spend two months at Rodney's getting out of debt and applying to schools. Rodney is an old friend from summer camp, and we've recently gotten back in touch. He's offered to basically give me his room in a big 2BR on the West Side while he's visiting family. It affords me the opportunity to work and get out of debt while applying to schools, leaving very little "financial footprint." The apartment is fine—a basic, relatively spacious, modern room in a city-owned complex near the West Side Highway. The location is key. Actually, the apartment smells weird—straight bachelors live here, pre—*Queer Eye*. To them, decorating means *Blade Runner* posters and gray wall-to-wall carpeting. Still, it's free. And it's in the West Village. Taylor's Bakery replaces the B train as my new best friend. I live on muffins and split pea soup as I focus on getting myself set up for the following year.

I've decided to apply to both graduate and undergrad programs, since I still am without a bachelor's degree. After a lot of research and thought, I choose NYU's Gallatin School (where I can get a BA without spending two years surrounded by twenty-year-olds), Brown (for playwright guru Paula Vogel), UCSD, and Juilliard. Juilliard is a long shot—they only take three writers a year, and the program is entirely free—but I figure, what the hell? I am now totally convinced that school is the right thing for me. I've thought of little else since hearing the words ("Eat meat. And apply to grad school.") in Vermont. It feels so right. With a school program, I will be able to give myself more options—a new skill set, a new community, new opportunities. Not to mention a temporary break from the survival game. Indeed, a few years in school—either undergrad, to finally get the BA, or one of the graduate-level writing programs—will help me to reconfigure everything. What I need right now: less survival, more laboratory.

My friends in New York are glad to have me back, even if they're wary of the new boyfriend who "lured me away" and some of the things he says, like "I don't believe in private money," and, when we fight, "Who is this *I*? I don't even *have* a self." What they don't see is how sweet he is to me, how we make each other laugh, and how much I've needed this warm, funny, sincere, totally authentic person who has about a thousand and one nicknames for me and cooks and holds me all night every night—at least, when he's not with his dad in Jersey. Sometimes, even when I want to let go of Noah, I feel glued to him. I do not yet know if this is healthy glue or bad toxic glue, but I want to stay and find out. So despite what I see as a difference in cultural expectations (where I come from, living in a van is not a badge of merit), we're trying to make it work. We love each other.

During this period, I temp at a management-consulting firm in Midtown, slowly getting out of debt and establishing some boundaries around money. I spend most nights with Noah seeing movies, eating cheap meals, and holding each other close. Sometimes, to be a good girlfriend, I take the PATH to Jersey and he comes and picks me up in Hoboken, but as I explain to him, it's less fun to hook up at someone's dad's house than in my own room, even if it's not really mine. And spending the night in Noah's sleeping bag in Jersey—he doesn't have his own room—involves buying cheap clothes at Strawberry in Grand Central Station at 8 A.M. on my way in to the office so that no one will think I'm a slut. We spend the entire winter like this.

Just before Christmas, Rodney's roommate asks to have the room back so that he can sublet to his brother, who should rightfully be living there anyway. Rodney has no plans to come back to New York, and thus no power to defend my temporary tenancy. And so I am once again on the prowl. I find a Williamsburg sublet from the sister of a friend of the women's health activist I've met through a group called "Sacred Harlots." I leave work early on a Thursday to check out her space and am charmed by the easy walk from the L train to Eleventh Street, all the more so when I see the space itself. Two days before New Year's Eve—my first with Noah—I move in.

....

118 North 11th Street, Brooklyn

This is a Bertolucci film waiting to happen. There are four gorgeous lesbians plus a small cat and an open-door bathroom policy—which just means, with five people in the house, if you need to pee and someone's in the tub, you are empowered to knock, enter, and do your thing. The women who live in the loft are all artists and filmmakers and poets. There is hand-laid Moroccan tile in the commons room. The antique tub is exquisite, as is most of the rest of the spacious once-industrial but now fully residential living space. And Williamsburg in 1997 is more like a college town on a river than the hipster Disneyland it will become in just a few short years. We're across the street from the Brooklyn Brewery, which we learn has free tastings on Sundays. Not too interesting to me since I don't drink beer, but very interesting to Noah, who sees all things culinary as scientific experiments, delicate chemistry. Oh yeah, and free beer.

I fall in love with the urban poetry of the warehouses

along Wythe Street, Oznot's Dish (a restaurant that looks like Ali Baba's secret cave), the L Café, and the tiny health food store. This is where I want to stay. I start looking to see if I can, even though my income is still meager and getting out of debt is the first priority. I *almost* take a 1BR floor-through for $600 on Metropolitan but my dear friend Trajal says, "Six hundred dollars! And you're living month to month with no savings account and waiting to hear from grad schools? How are you going to commit to six hundred dollars?" So I let it go and keep looking for shares. (Oh, Trajal, had we only known.)

When the loft sublet ends, I'm bereft. Not only because I haven't found a new place to go, but also because this is the best place I have been so far. I derive comfort from the big airy kitchen, the brightly colored tiles in the commons room, the high ceilings and amply sized bedroom. This is exactly how and where I want to live. And I'm tired of having to keep looking, keep moving, keep myself together and out of the way. I'm exhausted! I want to stay here! Is it an act of protest or nihilism or just plain acting-out when I can't find the next place?

I've been looking at shares, mostly from ads posted outside the L Café or the health food store on Bedford, without much luck since letting go of the $600 floor-through. January isn't a great time to move. People are mostly settled in the winter months; they look for subletters when it's warm and they themselves can travel or pursue creative opportunities out of town. My belongings have been in storage since San Francisco, so I travel lightly. But I'm exhausted and I want to land. And yet Trajal is right—with graduate school on the horizon, I'm not really in a position to get my own place or take on a lot of overhead. In fact, I have just enough for rent each month—and certainly not for a first month/last month security deposit. All of these sound like excuses. And they are excuses. Because I'm about to do something weird.

With my grad school applications in the mail, mustering whatever hope I can for the future, I wonder, What would happen if I just coast? I spend the month of March couch-surfing.

....

"Couch-Surf"

To "couch-surf" is to stay with someone, usually for free, and sleep on his or her couch. It is called "couch-surfing" because you're riding a wave. You can't stay with any one person long enough for him or her to get sick of you. Furthermore, there is a delicate balance between roommate and guest, because you are not paying actual rent and thus you have no rights. And yet, you're more than a guest, which means the person you are staying with does not ask what your favorite foods are or take special pains to help you feel comfortable. Theoretically, he or she wants you to find something else and leave. But he or she cares about you. If he or she did not care, you would not have been invited to stay in the first place. I spend much of my couch-surf time trying to be invisible—and indeed this is what rescues me from "coasting." I think you cannot coast very effectively when you do not simultaneously have someone with money somewhere willing to bail you out should things get too dire. I have no such someone, and thus my survival instincts kick in.

March goes like this: a week with my mother in Detroit (Not a successful visit. Note to self: refrain from seeing Marilyn when you are ungrounded and without a stable home.), a few days at Noah's dad's 1BR in northern New Jersey (we share the sleeping bag and Noah cooks, but his dad wonders, Why is your overage girlfriend sleeping on my floor?), a week with Joanna in the West Village, and so on until... Diane, a new friend I've recently met through some volunteer work for a breast cancer organization, calls with news. She has seen a flyer at a dance studio. A dancer in Park Slope is looking for a roommate ASAP, and the room is cheap. I haul my ass out to the South Slope one night to take a look, and it's lovely—which means affordable and clean with a bathtub and closet. At last, I have a home!

....

431 16th Street, Brooklyn

The south end of Park Slope is mostly middle class and residential in 1997. And it's delightful. There's a movie theater and a muffin store within walking distance from the apartment, which is sandwiched in between the South Slope and Windsor Terrace. There's an old Irish bar on the corner and a bagel shop that makes a mean sourdough waffle, as Noah and I will happily learn. Our building is a small but well-kept brownstone, which I'm told was once a nun's residence. There are nine apartments in the building—one on the ground floor and two per floor after that. We're 4L.

Krista, an Austrian dancer with a bad dye job, has been living here for roughly two years while on a student visa.

Lately, she doesn't go out much. I think she used to do a lot of things that she no longer does. I think she used to dance every day. Or go to class. Or see friends. But since getting injured a year ago, she stays home watching figure skating on the TV in her bedroom, with the door closed, and eating prepackaged luncheon meats, which both Noah and I think are bad for her chi. She has a subscription to *Playboy,* which arrives in brown wrapping once a month, and much later Noah will confess that she asked him out on a date after I moved out. (He, in fact, went on said date.) But for the moment, she is nice enough. We do not become friends. But I don't care. She's quiet and pleasant, and the apartment offers small, sweet, affordable respite. I pay $400 a month. My room is just as small as the room on West Ninth Street four years ago—and like that one has a beautiful built-in closet. Krista also gives me full owner-ship of the living room, since her own bedroom is roughly the size of both rooms combined—and then some. I put my books and desk in the living room, and appropriate the futon—already in the bedroom. Noah and I push it against the wall during the day and unroll it each night. My bed-room has one strange quirk: a square cutout in the wall, like a window without the glass, looking into the living room. I hang a curtain and ignore it. Noah points out, though, almost every time we have sex: "Dude, there's a hole in the wall. You should really do something about that."

Noah and I get my stuff out of the storage space it's been residing in since Wes put it there (the week we were medi-tating at the Buddhist place in California and Wes took a new roommate). And the beautiful, kind Noah Stern car-ries each and every box up each and every flight of stairs, saying, "Why do you have so many books?" but obliging nonetheless.

Park Slope feels different to me than it did two years earlier. Maybe it's the fact that we're on the complete other end of the neighborhood, much closer to the massive park with all of its wonders, as well as a bakery with genius scones and buttermilk biscuits good enough to make Noah over-look his distrust of wheat. There are so many things I like here: the swans in the park (Noah calls the water they live in "Lake Duck and Swan"), my local bagel store and tiny post office, the long rambling walks I take from our neigh-borhood across the avenues and down. For some reason, this spring the south end of Park Slope is just right.

I get a job working four days a week as the personal assistant to a film executive in TriBeCa. Okay, so it's the Finance Guy I used to date at twenty-one. He has lured me away from my temp agency saying, "You'll hate work-ing for me—I'm a dick, all my assistants say so—but I'll give you plenty of time to do your own thing and the hours are flexible." And he's right. On all counts. He is absolutely a dick. But the hours *are* flexible, the salary generous, and the working conditions agreeable. Four days a week, I sit in his luxury apartment in TriBeCa while he's out of town on a consulting job. I answer his phones, open his mail, pay his bills, balance his accounts, and manage all of his cor-respondence and travel arrangements. I even send flow-ers to his girlfriend when they fight. (He's conveniently forgotten that we used to date.) On the days that I work, I work hard. On other days, I sit in his apartment, copying his CDs, and raiding the fridge. I even use the bathtub. All in all, it's a perfect situation, and it saves me from having to go full-time and salaried at the management-consulting firm.

Most weekends Noah is with me as we explore Park Slope together, sneaking into the local movie theater, spending our money at the health food store instead. Noah cooks brilliant meals in my kitchen, which I think of as our kitchen. We celebrate our first anniversary in Vermont by breaking up and then deciding to stay together after all.

Two months after moving into Sixteenth Street, I find out that I've been accepted to the Lila Acheson Wallace American Playwrights Program at Juilliard, and my plans for the next few years are decided. I'm sitting in the Finance Guy's home office reconciling his American Express bill, amazed that this man can spend so much money in a strip club, when I stop to check my voice mail (the pre–cell phone era). There is a strange message from a voice I don't yet recognize: "Hello, Brooke. This is Christopher Durang. I love your play *Wonderland,* and I'd like you to meet Marsha Norman so that we can talk about bringing you to Juilliard." I'm delirious. (Christopher Durang? What? I love *your* plays, all of them, and you can bring me anywhere you want!)

I take the bus to Jersey that night and tell Noah the good news. He doesn't really know what Juilliard is, but he seems sort of happy for me. "If we're together in two years," I promise, "you can decide our next move. But for now, I am in New York . . . at Juilliard." It is a dream come true. The playwrights program accepts roughly three students a year. I cannot believe that I will be one of them.

I grew up hearing about The Juilliard School. It is the one place my mother wanted to go and couldn't—and continued to mythologize. ("Juilliard" and "Tiffany's" sounded a little similar, the way Marilyn talked about them. Juilliard was the absolute best, like Saks and Tiffany's, and again, nothing very bad could happen to you here.) As an actor, I learned that Juilliard was considered the finest training possible. I auditioned for the school's acting program once, when I was twenty years old and itching to leave college. I wanted professional training in the theater, and so as a lark, without telling anyone, I worked on a contemporary and a classical monologue and showed up ready. The audition was pleasurable, actually, involving a workshop with the late John Stix, and also I ran into this girl whom I'd been mistaken for at parties in Chicago, the friend of a friend, everyone said we looked alike. . . . Anyway, I didn't get in. But the experience is part of what led me to Providence in 1989 to study with Anne Bogart. It clarified something, showed me the kind of life and education that I wanted. Now I'm going to Juilliard after all, as a playwright and not an actress, to answer a question that I'd asked almost a decade earlier. The entire experience feels ordained. And finally, I feel, there is some order to the search.

After a summer of office work and free concerts in Prospect Park, I start graduate school. Conceived and cooperatively led by Marsha Norman and Christopher Durang, the Juilliard playwrights program is essentially a master class, more like an apprenticeship or a fellowship than the kind of academic program in which I'd have to write papers or take courses on theater history and theory. Marsha and Christopher want this to be collegial—and it is. We are treated like peers. Upon entry, I promise myself to put everything else aside and focus entirely on this one thing, becoming a real playwright. Much to my surprise the choice to focus my energy and limit my attention bears fruit. In fact, it's as if every other creative skill I've been cultivating (acting, dance, performance art, etc.) has coalesced into this one path, making me a better writer.

But it's amazing—as soon as I set this goal, every possible obstacle raises its head. For one thing, Noah doesn't understand my devotion to the theater or to the fellowship program. When I get free tickets to shows on Broadway and invite him, he asks, "Are there naked chicks? Otherwise, I'm not going."

The more insidious and troubling obstacle, though, is Marilyn, whose health has begun a monumental decline. The kidney that she received ten years earlier has failed, and she's back on dialysis; plus, her diabetes is out of control. She's eleven years older than she was in 1986, when she was last on dialysis, and a hundred times more delicate. My mom and grandma want me to be more available to them, to come home—if not forever, then at least for extended trips—to see and take care of her. I say no.

And here's the thing about that no. Because it is not said lightly, or with disregard for the seriousness of her situation. I have finally gotten myself on solid ground—finally—after years of postrape wandering and therapy and fear. And this educational opportunity at Juilliard will not wait. If I were to take any kind of leave of absence, I would not be able to return. Moreover, the whole thing is fraught because of the tenor of our relationship, the way in which Marilyn has always felt more like my child than my mother, and the ways in which I've been attempting, through therapy, since college really, to separate our identities and our paths. The issues surrounding my mom's health and my choice to take care of myself first are so intense and delicate that I can't do them justice here. Suffice to say, I do what I can to support her from afar and give her my love while prioritizing my own life, income, and education. Which means I stay in school and keep showing up for my assorted strange jobs. Meanwhile, I try to have the relationship I can with her. There is guilt—so much so that I don't even recognize it as "guilt"—it just feels like the white noise that's always been present whenever my mother is involved. And there is drama. It is rare that we have a phone conversation that doesn't end in a screaming match, tears, or horrible accusations. But we love each other deeply, and we both keep trying. From time to time, at work or at school, I get messages on my voice mail from Marilyn saying, "It's your mother, I'm on death's doorstep." But she generally sounds more angry than sick, so I wait a few hours before calling her back. Much later she will deny ever having made these calls, but I know from the number of times I fight about them with Noah (who says I am too hard on her), or the therapy sessions that follow, or both, that the calls are indeed real. My therapist advises, "The next time she says she's dying, ask her if she'd like you to call 911."

In my work life, I've moved from management consulting into the finance sector, at one of the enormous banking firms on Broadway, and on the days that I'm not in school, I sit at various desks, answering phones. The work is mindless, but I get a lot of time to myself. Often, I'm reading and writing and drinking coffee while taking messages and doing expense reports for the "bosses" who all look like people I could have gone to high school with in the Midwest. The wardrobes, certainly, are similar.

Three days a week of office work does not bring in quite enough money. So I take a regular babysitting job for a family near school with two adorable daughters. Sometimes Noah will join me at the job and chase the little girls around the apartment pretending to be "The Bad Teeth Monster" or a crazed pizza delivery guy. The little girls run through their apartment screaming with delight. And later, I put them to bed and read from their *Harry Potter* books, thinking, Someday Noah and I will have kids, and it will be just like this. We've been together for almost two years at this point, and although we talk about marriage and children, I know neither of us is ready yet. Noah doesn't even have his own place! And I'm in the middle of my first year of graduate work. Babies will have to wait.

In addition to temping and babysitting, I do things like throw an impromptu stoop sale or teach weekend writing workshops to earn extra cash. I'm becoming more and more adept at making money. And I'm developing faith, which is an entirely new thing. I'm constantly tired. And still mostly broke. But I know where I need to be, doing the work I need to do, and finally after years of living this way, I know it's going to be okay.

In early 1998 it becomes clear that the commute from Sixteenth Street in the Slope up to Lincoln Center and my babysitting job on the Upper West Side is taking too long and costing too much. I decide to look for something closer. Although I've loved living in this apartment, and in this neighborhood, it has become a hassle. And Kyra, a new friend I've met—on the Marianne Williamson Web site, no less—is looking to move out of her boyfriend's place. We decide to look for something together, ideally in lower Manhattan, which I have missed. And this is how we both meet Stella.

I show up to the open house at a small 2BR on Broome

Street, near Orchard, ready to convince the landlords what spectacular tenants Kyra and I will be. The landlords aren't around, and the open house is just me and one other girl. The apartment is both small and dark with an odd smell coming from the nearby markets. It's not quite close enough to Chinatown for fish but . . . it smells like fish. Living in Brooklyn for the last two years has spoiled me— bigger rooms, more pleasant odors. Still, I tell myself, it's Broome and Orchard, and the Lower East Side has always been a favorite destination; I want this apartment. I only hope that without a competitive application (which, let's be honest, we won't have—I'm a graduate student without a steady paycheck and Kyra is a freelancer) we still have a shot. I tentatively hold the fancy "application package" that Kyra and I have made—an art project, nestled in a Kate's Paperie folder, designed to make us look better than we are because Kyra and I are both convinced that our energies, if properly aligned, will open doors.

To lease an apartment in New York City (not a share), you need proof of income, bank statements, pay stubs, and, very often, a "guarantor." A guarantor is someone related to you, with money, who promises to be responsible for the rent if you can't pay. The process is as fierce and intense as applying to graduate school. Our "package" reflects our mutual creativity and our commitment to be good tenants. It also reflects the fact that I don't yet have steady income. I've included pay stubs from my temp jobs and a letter from my babysitting clients. Kyra includes a letter from her employer and some of her freelance writing clips. Neither of us has savings or a credit card or a guarantor. But we both believe in miracles, and so we're going to wing it.

God sends Stella, who has a real job and good credit. Moreover, she's a go-getter. A recent graduate of a top art and design program, she plans to work days in Midtown and then lease an art studio and spend her weekends painting. When I meet her at that Broome Street open house, she turns to me and says, "This place sucks. I'm going to look at stuff in Williamsburg tomorrow—do you want to come?"

The next morning, I meet her for breakfast and we talk for over an hour—art school, theater school, boyfriends, "making it" in New York—the whole nine yards. She takes me with her to meet the real estate agent, who shows us apartments in both Williamsburg and nearby Greenpoint, two up-and-coming neighborhoods in the northern part of Brooklyn, nearer to Queens. By the end of the day, I've fallen madly in love with everything about Stella—her art degree, her tattoos, and her matter-of-fact approach to real estate—and we have signed the lease on a 3BR in Greenpoint. I call Kyra and explain the whole thing, suggesting that the three of us live together. I convince her that the Greenpoint apartment, while not huge, is definitely big enough and—best yet—the rent will be ridiculously low. Kyra agrees to give it a shot, sight unseen, and a week later we move into what Noah already calls "La Casa Tres Girlies."

....

680 Manhattan Avenue, Brooklyn

There are a few things that make this move different from the others. One, it's the first time *ever* that I'm moving by choice and not necessity. I want to live closer to school, and even though it's still Brooklyn, I have reduced my commute by more than half without significantly raising my expenditures. In fact, with three of us in the apartment, my share is just *under* $400, which means, it is less than Park Slope! Second, I looked for an apartment on my own, casually, and found one with relatively no hassle in roughly one month's time. Next, and possibly most important yet, this is the first apartment I will move into that feels like it is mine—no already-tenured roommates to befriend or adjust to, no stepping over someone's disgusting faux-velvet armchair, handmade milk-crate plant holder or ugly coffee table, no abandoned bed to adopt or kitchen to fit my groceries into. Everything is new. Paint is fresh. Wires are still hanging. A new stove, a new refrigerator, newly sanded wood floors. It is, in all ways, a fresh start. My apartment with Wes was clean and freshly painted when we moved in, but this is different. Maybe because Fifth Avenue always felt like his—he found it, he decorated, he made the rules. Or because this place has just been renovated—sawdust is still on the floor—it is the first genuine blank slate.

Last, and perhaps most vital, I'm on the lease. And it makes a difference. Previously, I wouldn't have said this, but now I can see an increased sense of ownership and pride, responsibility even—just because it's my lease. Or, mine and Stella's. With a room rented to Kyra. And on the Saturday we move in, we all agree: The whole thing is a gift from the gods.

We are a motley moving crew. Stella has a truck, so she is in charge. Kyra has a bunch of cute guys helping carry boxes. I have Noah, who tickles me in between every trip upstairs and is delighted to see that my room will be way more private than on Sixteenth Street. We carry bags, boxes, and furniture up the flights of stairs and then head for Oznot's Dish and an inaugural meal of roasted vegetables and curry. I wake up on that first morning still charmed by the smell of a freshly painted apartment, wondering, *What will happen here? And for how long?*

Greenpoint is a Polish neighborhood directly north of Williamsburg, and in 1998 still mostly undiscovered by hipsters. This will change. Despite the inconvenience of a subway line called the G—"G for ghetto train," Noah says—chic bars and boutique clothing stores will turn up within the next five years, and rents will hit record highs. But in 1998 it's still uncharted terrain to many. The local stores advertise their wares in Polish. And they sell things you can't buy in other places: kielbasa, pierogi, Naleczowianka spring water. Not that I eat any of that. But I enjoy the unfamiliar sounds and combinations of letters. It is not uncommon for strangers to address me in Polish on the street. A Polish Jew, I do look like I could be from the old country. Which I could be, of course, if history had been different. Suffice to say, in 1998 in Greenpoint, I get mistaken for a Pole, and I think it's cool. There is a video store across the street, stellar Thai food at the nearby Thai Café, and organic produce at the equally nearby Garden, a gourmet food store a few blocks closer to Queens. On the Saturdays that I'm not at Juilliard, I roam up and down Manhattan Avenue and sometimes over to Williamsburg, exploring all this goodness. I am charmed to find myself in a neighborhood that I have no history in, nothing to remind me of the past, no previous narrative. I am free.

And there is plenty of goodness at La Casa. We are all

three artists and vegetarians. (Even though the vision in 1996 told me to eat meat, I won't be able to integrate that for another decade.) One of my friends says, "It's like an apartment full of the three graces," and mostly it is. Stella is a visual artist who works in graphic design, Kyra is a writer who works in new media, and I'm in the theater, at Juilliard. We make coffee in the mornings and black beans and rice at night. We (mostly) like the same kind of music (although Stella has a strange aversion to jazz). And we're blessed when Stella starts hanging her art on the walls— Mark Rothko—esque color washes, urban landscapes, ribbons of color that melt into other ribbons of color. It is a beautiful space. I will live here for over two years, happily. Stella will live here even longer. Kyra will move back to Manhattan as soon as she possibly can. But all and all, it is a good home, one in which respect and creativity are both plentiful, both encouraged.

That summer, I win a playwriting award that takes me to the Denver Center Theater and gives me a little cash. It's my first paid gig as a playwright and also the first break I've had in some time—a break from earning money, a break from New York, and a break from Noah, who has lately been saying that he might want "space."

More on that. Noah has rented a room of his own in an apartment in Williamsburg not so far from me. This is a great turn of events for him. After a few years of living in Jersey, I think he relishes the freedom and also the joy of living around people his own age. It is something I have been encouraging since we first got back to New York and he moved in with his dad, insisting that he didn't need his own place. ("Listen," he said, "in many cultures people live with their parents and grandparents well into their twenties, if not longer." To which I replied, "Yes, but you don't live in those cultures. You live in New Jersey.") Although it's totally appropriate and understandable, I am nonetheless hurt when he says, "I moved to New York for you, and I don't know who I am here without you. . . . I need some room to figure it out." Stunned, I say, "Are you breaking up with me?" He insists that he's not. But he wants to have adventures. I ask, "Do you want to see other people? Are we both doing that?" He says, "I don't know, no, maybe . . . Follow your heart." I'm not sure what "follow your heart" means. I want structure. After a week of sleepless nights and painful conversations that go nowhere, I announce that I'm going to New Mexico after my residency in Denver. Alone. The way I see it, if he needs to explore who he is "without me," let him. Meanwhile, I will travel and do some exploring of my own.

I arrange to spend the month after my Denver residency house-sitting for Grace, who has moved to Albuquerque. She'll be embarking on a monthlong camping-trip honeymoon with her new husband, leaving their sweet little house in my care. I can't wait for a whole month on my own in the magnificent desert-meets-mountain landscape of northern New Mexico. I plan to devote myself entirely to writing and meditation. It's true that Grace and I have had our share of problems, but equally true that we always work them out. "We rock long distance," she says. And this generous offer of hers, for me to live in her house, is the answer to my prayers.

It's hard to be without a car in Albuquerque, but I do okay on foot and riding the bus (which does, in fact, stop service at 8 P.M., leaving me housebound). It's an enormous gift to have this sweet, small, light-filled house to

myself, not to mention unstructured time and the space to
investigate. I meditate twice daily. I give up caffeine. I cook
all of my own meals and take cool, lavender-scented baths
in the afternoon reading Grace's books on herbalism and
natural childbirth. I go hiking in the Jemez Mountains with
a local women's hiking group that I have found through a
flyer in the health food co-op (a fantastic group—the hik-
ers are way more butch, and way more adept, than me, but
they are patient when I need to take rests on the mountain
and kindly invite me back). I also hike with my neighbors,
ex–forest rangers from Montana who hit the mountain at
sunset and know their trails. I'm going to turn thirty in
six months. And I think, Who do I want to be? What kind
of writer? What kind of woman? And what do I want to
create? What are my investments and where are my attachments? I ask these questions, and then wait and listen for
answers.

The more I "explore" a life without Noah, the more I
know I want a life with him. Strangely, I am never more
certain than when I'm flirting with Noah Two (really—his
name is also Noah, something I comment on immediately).
Noah Two is a yogi painter I've been spending time with
since arriving in town. I meet him on the very day that I've
written to Noah One, telling him "I am following my heart,
but you don't have to worry—no one else is you." The brief
flirtation with Noah Two (it would be overstating the case
to call it an actual "affair." Besides, no one is married—I
can barely get a dating commitment out of Noah One)
ends with my toes in his mouth and the sure and steady
knowledge that the only guy I want is the one at home in
Brooklyn. I tell Noah Two (once I remove my toes from
his mouth) that I'm staying faithful to my boyfriend, and I

get back to the business of writing, promising myself, "no more distractions."

Two months earlier, as my first year at Juilliard came to a close, I asked Marsha Norman if we might meet over drinks to discuss my work. I asked, "What should I focus on?" Marsha's response: "I don't know where you come from. And I'd like to see you write a play about that." It's a hard assignment. Where *do* I come from? I come from Marilyn, who comes from Ida, the matriarch with Emilio Pucci dresses, long fingernails, and more common sense or work ethic than anyone I have ever met. I come from dinners at the Ritz Carlton with my mom and The Archduke and from the all-night fights that followed, where dishes and glassware got thrown across the room as if they were percussive instruments, keeping time with every accusation. I come from a house of music. From listening to my mom play Mozart with her eyes closed. And I come from a house of fashion, sitting through "trunk showings" with Marilyn and the designers she represented. (I was the only eight-year-old in the Detroit suburbs who could speak on Giorgio Armani's fall line.) But I have not been in any of those houses since I was eighteen years old—over a decade ago. And now I feel like I come more from Avenue A. From the poppy-seed cake and dance workshops, downtown sublets and unmatched clothes, care of Salvation Armani. Where *do* I come from? I start writing about my childhood: which means Marilyn. Mostly about her marriages. First to my dad, who I barely remember, and then to The Archduke, who has been dying of a brain tumor in a nursing home without her. And then I write— really and most movingly, at least for me—about how much Marilyn loved being a mother. She claimed the happiest time of her life was when she was pregnant with me. I call the play *Mom's Lap* (this title will later change, and the play itself fall apart) because once I had this notion that nothing very bad could happen when I was a little girl in Marilyn's lap. Marilyn always made herself available to me—physically, emotionally, and spiritually. And while I've certainly taken distance from the physical Marilyn, I have a deep respect for the way in which she took care of and mothered me. My mother always let me know that I was loved. I was wanted—which means planned—and loved.

And despite our fighting, Marilyn and I still tell each other how much we love one another on a regular basis. Mostly we've agreed to disagree. She wants to see more of me, and I want more autonomy to focus entirely on school and establishing some kind of ground or base. It seems like the only way I can be of use in the world is to be of use to myself, which means setting up the structures by which I will be able to support myself fully, live abundantly, express my creative gifts—things that she herself never did. And she admits this. In more than one late-night phone call, my mom acknowledges that she never left home—apart from marrying—and might not entirely understand what I'm up to. The ability to leave home is both psychic as well as physical. In fact, she concedes, the psychic leave taking is the more lasting of the two.

Noah visits for the Fourth of July, and I tell him the abridged story of Noah Two, ending with the truth: "I wanted him to be you."

He is unimpressed with the revelation that he's the one who matters. And ambivalent when I ask, "Can we take the next step?"

He says, "I don't care about the other guy. I'm not jealous. I just want to know if you sucked his dick."

"What are you talking about?" I ask.

"It's a simple question."

"I won't answer. It's not important."

"I think it's important."

"But you're the one I want! Can we talk about us?"

But we don't talk about us. And I'm devastated when,
after a long and strange road trip with strangers to see Lilith
Fair in the desert, Noah abruptly takes off for Los Angeles
(by train, to see his mother) days earlier than we'd planned.
I watch him go, angry and sad. He was the one who wanted
"space." I wanted stability and a sound commitment. I did
what he said, following my heart, while we were (like Ross
and Rachel) "on a break"—and now he's leaving!

The insomnia comes back with a vengeance. Since
meeting Noah, I've slept beautifully, soundly, through the
night. But now, alone in Grace's house, I stay awake until
dawn, waiting to feel safe enough to sleep. Every noise is an
intruder. I explore all permutations of Sleepytime Tea and
valerian root. (Everyone says valerian is the shit, but when
I take it—after a "weed walk" with the local herbalist school,
digging the valerian out of the ground myself and cooking it up on the stovetop—it has the reverse effect. Like
the time I took No-Doz in high school, Valerian leaves
me wired and sloppy, as if there's this enormous cocoon
made of fog surrounding my outsides and a very tight little
wired wide-awake person inside.) I become intimate with
my middle-of-the-night fears. Before the summer's end, I
will have befriended and conquered them. But first I have
to face each—head on.

In the middle of one very long night, I call a local

rape-crisis hotline. I say, "It happened five years ago, but this is the first time I'm living in a house, outside of New York City, alone. It's quiet, and then not quiet; I don't trust the sounds, or the lack of sounds. I stay up all night, every night, not sleeping."

The phone volunteer suggests, "It sounds like post-traumatic stress disorder. Have you ever thought about that?" Psychic healing for deeply buried rage, yes. But PTSD, no. She says, "It might just take time for you in new places. . . . You may have to acclimate, get to know the surroundings and create safety for yourself before you can relax, let your guard down, and sleep." She asks me to describe what I hear, and then, together, we deconstruct each noise. (Traffic here sounds really different from traffic in New York City.) She encourages me to talk through whatever thoughts are keeping me awake until I've forgotten to be afraid and remembered instead that I'm really tired. I can't believe that after five years these symptoms are still connected to the attack. Identifying that they are helps me release them. And learning about PTSD helps me identify what to release and how to talk to myself when I'm scared. And, of course, there's Penney, who still does sessions with me over the phone while I'm out of town. She suggests that the sleepless nights might be a psychic discharge and that this time alone is good for my overall healing. She is right.

I pretend that my time in New Mexico is a spiritual retreat. I continue to meditate and write every day. I cook healthy food, take walks in the late afternoons and, in the evenings, sit on the porch watching the sunset. I give up caffeine and conquer my fear of being alone in the middle of the night. Sometimes I can spend an entire day without talking. Finally my mind becomes quiet. By August I've finished a first draft of my play and am ready to go back to Brooklyn. I don't see light shooting out of people's heads anymore, but I am starting to realize the point of it all is to see that light in the world or, maybe, bring that light to the world. And *that* I can do. Anyone can, really. Finding the light—and then bringing that light to the world—seems to me, to be the point of everything. And just like all the healers promised, stabilizing my physical reality, establishing a home and a solvent bank account, is the key to the light. At least it is for me. The light can only be as effective as the vessel through which it travels. I am strengthening my vessel.

I return home in August, surprisingly happy to see Greenpoint, Brooklyn. Noah has been crashing in my room, having moved out of his first apartment and in the throes of looking for his second. My first night back I press him, "Can we move in together? Are you still in love with me? Did you miss me when I was gone?" He won't take a stand. I push. We fight. ("I just want to know if you sucked that guy's dick.") He finds a new share in a Williamsburg house near the third L stop, with four art students, all of whom smoke inordinate amounts of marijuana—he says it's like living with a pack of fairies. I think in his mind this is a good thing. Again, he won't break up with me, but he's stopped saying that he's in love. He makes fun of me, calling me "Little Bird" because I want "to nest." And he starts getting high every day, growing a marijuana plant in his closet and ignoring the mice, which are also in his closet. He forgets when we've made dates or shows up late when he's not blowing me off completely. I accuse him of addiction. He accuses me of my own addictions—to coffee and sugar, insisting they're the same thing and I'm a hypocrite. "Coffee is not the same as pot!" I say. But I give it up anyway, stubbornly, to prove that I can.

That fall, I start school again. And on Christmas Eve, Noah and I break up. I know it's for the best, for both of us, but that doesn't make it any easier. Now that we're actually separating, he admits that he *is* still in love with me. In fact, he says, "I look at you and see the woman I want to spend the rest of my life with, and then I think, Holy shit, I'm twenty-five years old. I'm not ready for that!" Maybe that's where the pot smoking comes into play. But the thing is, I *am* ready. I'm turning thirty in a few months and want to settle down. We both know we have to let go. We even talk about breaking up for a year, in order to see if we'll get married later on—but no one can say what "later on" will hold. Deal making is not permitted in these circumstances. The Infinite Universe demands: Just let go.

"What do you want to do in the world without me?" I ask.

He says, "I want to do a lot of drugs and have anonymous sex."

How does one respond to that? Is he joking? Something tells me he isn't.

I say, "I don't want to try to be friends during this period. I don't want to see you. I don't want to know where you are." So once we break up, we drop all contact—until we start hooking up again later.

The weekend we break up, between Christmas and New Year's, we just cry and hold each other, and on the day he actually leaves, I feel like I've lost a limb. I can't eat or sleep. It's the most awful feeling yet.

I spend New Year's Eve in Montreal with a divorced

minister I've met through my friends in Vermont and her two small children. We watch Kevin Kline movies—again and again and again—in order to heal my broken heart. And it works. Kevin Kline is the only force of nature who can quiet my heart and get me to stop crying. (The Maurice Chevalier—esque accent in *French Kiss* does the trick every time.) It's freezing cold in Montreal, so I don't see much of the town, and I arrive back in New York a few days later to discover that Kevin Kline is a guest teacher for the winter semester at Juilliard. The Infinite Universe is paying attention.

Kyra moves out, and Sondra moves in. Sondra has a boyfriend who she sort of "stays with"—which means, while she has a bag or two in the room that used to be Kyra's, and she pays rent and utilities, I only see her once in the entire four months she lives at La Casa. Stella and I are mostly on our own. This is when we become close. We do Kundalini yoga in the living room in the mornings and meditate at night. We rent movies. We go dancing. She's my primary ally in this new chapter of both creativity and single life as we compare notes on love, art, and Prana.

I turn thirty at the Humana Festival of New American Plays in Louisville, Kentucky, where they are performing my ten-minute *Dancing with a Devil* in an evening titled "Life Under 30." The Humana Festival is like the Sundance of new plays: Each year roughly six are produced and then performed in rotation, and on the "Big Weekend," in March or April, all of the artistic directors and literary managers from around the country come to see what's often considered the "crème de la crème." "Life Under 30" consists of eight ten-minute plays by writers thirty and under, directed and acted by directors and actors who are all also thirty and under. I'm still at Juilliard, and now, since becoming single, ridiculously prolific. It's one of my best birthdays yet. Better still after a brief affair with the sound designer, the first person I have kissed since breaking up with Noah. (He calls me "a little blonde thing" and I say, "It's from a bottle.") I return from Louisville, grateful to be back in Greenpoint, grounded and loving my home for what feels like the first time in a long time.

Penney says this is when the real shifts start occurring. Without Noah, I am getting down to business. And although I'm still sore—heartbroken, raw—the truth is, this feels like a holy time, a clearing. Yoga becomes a regular part of my life when my friend Monica has to go out of town and begs me to cover for her "karma yoga" (a nice way of saying work-study) shifts at Jivamukti Yoga Center. One night of "karma yoga" (cleaning the studio and folding blankets) affords me two free classes a week, and soon Jivamukti is a lifeline. I become physically strong for the first time in my life. Plus, turning thirty seems to have wiped out a lot of fear. It's as if someone has handed me the keys to a toolbox and somehow I know how to use each and every tool. The experiences of the past few years have finally accrued into a coherent whole, and apart from missing Noah—he haunts me—I feel great. Happy. Adult. Released.

When I graduate from Juilliard in May, my mother and grandmother come to New York to celebrate. They don't visit my apartment—after one trip to Brooklyn, Marilyn is not up for a second, even if it's an entirely different part of the borough. Still, this is our most successful and pleasant visit as she and Ida come to see my final project at school and then spend a Saturday afternoon at Avery Fisher Hall listening to Mozart. I think this is one of my mom's best days.

In the pictures, there we are: three small Jewish women with unnaturally blond hair, smiling. And the smiles are real.

That summer, I take a job fact-checking for *Working Mother* magazine, and I vow to get my creative life in order. I am one of the only students to graduate without an agent, and so I do what I can to polish each of my plays and prepare for the moment when someone wants to represent me. I do public, staged readings of each play, making sure the scripts are tight. And I wait.

I see Noah twice that summer, and both times we wind up kissing, then going back to my apartment where the next morning, after he leaves, I'm greeted by Stella and a raised eyebrow. (One of these evenings includes a visit to Nobu for sashimi and black cod, the best meal I've ever had.) Then Noah moves to Amsterdam, telling me clearly, over e-mail, that he never wants to be with me again. Ever. I'm devastated—really, really devastated—but determined to stay on a clear path. Besides, I don't believe him. The one thing I know is that Noah and I aren't over. Still, I start to date the owner of the local independent bookstore, who is also training to become a Buddhist monk and who has the same first name as me. It's charming when we're out together—Brooke and Brooks—but limited, as we both admit we're not falling in love. After a four-year break, I'm back in touch with Sam, who now claims to be in love with me himself, after all these years! "It's too late," I tell him. "I moved on. I'm still in love with Noah, my ex."

"What's he like?" asks Sam.

And I am forced to admit, "Tall, lanky, half-Jewish, and from New Jersey—like you."

That fall, my mother has her second kidney transplant,

and I fly back to Detroit to be with her. This recovery process is different from the first, thirteen years earlier. She's
way more delicate and less responsive; the previous two years
on dialysis have taken their toll. My family and I spend long
days in the hospital waiting for Marilyn to come through
her surgery. I can't even see her there—mostly unconscious
and ridiculously fragile, like a little doll—without getting
really upset. I call Stella from the pay phone at the hospital numerous times a day. She's been reading Caroline
Myss's *Anatomy of the Spirit* and she tells me to "unplug" from
the guilt, fear, and anger surrounding my mom, to love
my mom without the attendant feelings of desperation that
accompany her various illnesses. I try my best. But we are
talking about nearly thirty years of wiring, and there's a lot
to unplug from, namely the belief that I'm responsible for
my mom's health and her very right to be in the world. I
return to Brooklyn a few days later, exhausted but relieved
that Marilyn will be off dialysis, and hopefully feeling better. I want to feel better, too.

I go back to work at the magazine and back to writing. I spend Christmas alone in a French restaurant on
Spring Street, sobbing over Noah. It is the year anniversary of our breakup, and I miss him terribly. And then on
New Year's Eve, he calls. He's on his way back to New York
from Europe—via Florida—by bus. And he has a catering
job (already? I guess that's good news). He wants to see me
as soon as possible. And so, in January 2000, we start to
date. We've never really done that—dated. The experience
is new. Instead of immediately living together (or driving
across the country) we meet, spend a few days together,
and separate. We fight a lot. But neither of us wants to stay

apart for very long. So, once a month or so, Noah and I are together for a few days doing what we do—fucking, laughing, eating great meals, and watching science fiction films about the end of the world. After a few days, we fight and break up until we get back together three weeks later and start the whole cycle again. Each time I think it's going to be different. Each time it isn't.

The millennium comes and goes without any major bank crashes or New World visions (Noah was prepared). And I keep working. One magazine job turns into another, from *Working Mother* to the more alternative *Paper*. Life at La Casa is stable and good. Things with Noah are on, then off, then on again. And then, in April 2000, I receive a call informing me that I've won a playwriting award—I didn't even know I'd been nominated—and that the award comes with an enormous cash prize. At first I think this must be a joke. Who would be so cruel as to call with this absurd message? But when I call back to get the details, I realize it's no joke. I have $20,000 coming—as do two other playwrights—and we'll be given our awards and checks at a cocktail party at the Second Stage Theatre in one month's time.

Nothing like this has ever happened to me before. I have been working hard, with little to no support or acclaim, since starting Juilliard. And now fortune is smiling. I don't even know what to do with money, I think. (I will learn quickly.) For days after receiving the check—and drinking fancy Chardonnay at the reception—I hole up in my room, seemingly unable or unwilling to leave. I ask other playwrights who have won the same award, What did you do with the money? One paid off credit card debt, another shopped. Still another invested. It's an amazing array of options. And no judgments. The key is to make a choice with as much awareness as possible.

Previously, I've defined myself by lack. If I don't have money, then I will not have to make certain choices. I can't be held responsible. I walk into a restaurant and order the cheapest thing on the menu without ever asking the question, *What do I want?* I buy my clothing secondhand and then re-create and deconstruct the pieces into "Salvation Armani" finery (*Pretty in Pink* meets Desperately Seeking Prada). I've been living in small rooms in small apartments for as long as I can remember, adjusting myself to the circumstance, making lemonade whenever lemons are presented. (Thank you, Grandma Ida.) I've become so successful at living within my means that I have stopped asking myself, *What do I want?* And now, without these limitations, who will I be? In addition to the conceptual revolution that winning money has set off, there are a whole lot of strange ideas and magical thinking showing up in my thoughts: First. *don't tell anyone.* Second, *don't have too much fun.* I want to be responsible, I want to make solid choices, I don't want anyone taking the money away from me, and silently, secretly, I want to savor the sweetness of being rewarded—with enough humility that fortune won't desert me. Isn't magical thinking amazing? The deals we make with ourselves? The control we think we have?

Still, I want to make a well-considered plan. Travel? Quit the magazine and write until the funds run out? Invest? Throw a party? I know this money won't last forever or afford me every opportunity, so I ask, What will be most beneficial at this moment, this year? And what will support my writing? I decide to keep the day job while quietly and systemically "raising my bottom"—like an overall systems upgrade. I give notice in Greenpoint and decide to move back to Manhattan, thereby increasing my rent by a few hundred dollars a month. I buy some clothes (on sale) and take a few more cabs late at night. I eat my favorite food—sushi—at least once a week. And I allow myself to experience life, for the first time in a long time, with a financial cushion. Which means less edge. Which means I am sleeping really well. There is one more treasure in the treasure chest—news of the award has yielded my first playwriting agent, a woman whose taste I have long admired. And with this, I am in the game.

The lessons of the past few years have started to accrue. A base is now present where I used to have none, the elusive "grounding" I've been working on for years. Some combination of my work with Penney Leyshon plus the experience of a stable home and solvent bank account, graduate school, the incredibly painful work of letting go of Noah, and my growing commitment to writing has all come together to yield this miracle. And it's not the money, it's me. I'm finally becoming strong, in body and spirit. Thank God.

....

345 West Broadway

"Guys will treat us differently when they see where we live," says Emma, a young book editor and my new roommate. Emma and I met a year ago through mutual friends in publishing and immediately bonded over our shared passion for both Liz Phair and Jane Austen, becoming fast friends. After a late night out, during the Greenpoint years, I was

wont to crash on Emma's enormous velvet couch to avoid
the subway at 2 A.M. Emma is one of the few people I con-
fide in about the playwriting award because, let's face it, she
has money of her own. And knows how to use it. She is my
guide to good sushi, sample sales, and mojitos. So it's only
natural when she invites me to move in. Although I've been
looking for my own place, the chance to live with her, and
to live *here,* is just too good. And she's right about bringing guys home. When the elevator doors open onto the
massive full-floor, high-ceilinged, sunken-living-room
SoHo loft, they inhale slightly and they know: *You can't
treat these girls like trash. You might be allowed to make out with them, even
sleep over—but you better watch yourself.*

The loft (which I nickname "The Princess Apartment")
is one of those spaces you see on TV but don't believe real
people actually inhabit: sunken living room, high ceilings,
floor-to-ceiling built-in bookshelves, and an extraordinary wash of natural light every morning *and* every afternoon. My favorite part: a marble bathtub the size of a
small country. You could have eight of your friends in that
bathtub, and nothing improper would have to occur. My
room has a window looking directly onto the World Trade
Center towers. Emma's bedroom takes up over half the
square footage and contains a washer/dryer and an area we
refer to as "the studio." All the best boutiques are within a
two-block radius, along with a china shop, a leather shop,
and a very expensive bar. Around the corner is one of my
most favorite places, the bistro Lucky Strike. I always seem
to know someone who works at Lucky Strike—Julia, Josh,
Woody—and so I am there often, eating veggie burgers and
bread pudding with a late-night glass of Malbec.

Emma's father owns the loft, and so we live here paying

"maintenance" only: My share is $600 a month. This is only $50 more per week than living with two girls in Greenpoint, and my entire life improves the moment I move in. (The final months in Greenpoint were starting to feel a little like the Apocalypse when the building caught on fire, the gas was turned off, and the mice started showing up.) I make up the difference solely through the lack of subway fare or cabs. When you live in lower Manhattan, why not walk everywhere? Work, yoga, rehearsals, dinners . . . everything is close.

The first morning, I wake up and throw open the sliding Japanese doors that separate my room from the rest of the apartment. Light is spilling in through the big picture windows and bouncing off the amber-colored wooden floors, and I feel I have come home. This is heaven. I am never leaving.

Emma and I do a clean sweep of the place. We blend my things with hers, putting my books on the gorgeous built-in shelves, combining our dishes and glassware. We make lists of what we need and then enjoy a massive shopping trip at the nearby National Wholesale Liquidators. (I do have money but not yet enough to shop without care.) We share a closet (the size of many rooms that I have lived in prior) and clothes (hers are more expensive with actual designer names attached, but mine have vintage flair). We share basic groceries (but not specialty items as hers are gourmet and mine are either discount or vegan, neither of which Emma much cares for). We even throw a series of dinner parties for our growing community of shared friends. All in all, we have a blast. We hang out in the local Irish bar playing games. (Emma has a thing for darts, but I far prefer leaning over a pool table, asking some hot guy to show me how to hold the stick. And I am not even joking.)

We shop and dance and drink and play and share Victorian romance novels. What could be bad? We fight, too—like sisters—but I don't think it's a particularly bad sign. I just think, *She's family.*

Best yet, the loft becomes the center of our respective creative lives. Emma hosts book groups and writing workshops, while I have rehearsals and informal play readings here. Emma is particularly helpful with my work. She is astute and bright, used to dealing with the complexities of language and emerging trends in writing—in other words, a smarty-pants. Her insights, after reading or listening to any one of my plays, are the ones that help me most in "cracking" the story and developing its structure. We spend days talking about art and literature and theater. We value similar things in each—direct engagement, unapologetic desire, and magic. We read each other's books and see plays at theater companies who are, one by one, inviting me to take part in their writing groups and extended families. Together we lament over the trend toward both nihilism and misogyny in new American plays. We want to see female characters with real voices and character arcs—more than just "the slut" or "the mom" or "the victim"—rendered with the same complexity given to male characters. We want plays in which women appear and aren't punished for their gender or their sexual exploits. And I personally want someone to say something redemptive about the human condition without resorting to sentimentality or cliché. But the theater doesn't think so much of redemption. Or alternative narrative structures. One older, male artistic director says, after a reading of my most recent fare, "I feel like we were fucking, and I didn't come." To which I reply, "I did."

The thing is, I believe in creation. And I've noticed that most plays dealing with the tragic suffering of the human condition are written by people who haven't experienced that much of it themselves. People who have genuinely suffered, more often than not, want to laugh. So with Emma's support, and the support of my actor friends from Juilliard, I create work that delights me. I believe—I still believe—it's the only way.

And I'm lucky in that the work is received. By the fall of 2000, I'm doing "readings" and "workshops" of my plays everywhere from the local Soho Rep to the Royal Court Theatre in London. At home, I am invited to join writers' groups and participate in new work festivals, most specifically with a fledgling theater company run by recent Juilliard grads, Rising Phoenix Rep.

And I have a new play: *Smashing.* The story follows two twenty-one-year-old girls on a revenge trip to London, stalking a hot young novelist who has written an exposé about his affair with one of the girls. The girl in question, Abby, is his ideal. But there is a best friend, Clea, and really, it's her play all along. My agent calls this structure "a sleight of hand" because I want the audience to attach to Abby's charisma (just as Clea and the novelist do) but then realize (as Clea and the novelist must) that Abby is flawed, complicit in her own objectification. Clea is the real hero, the "stealth protagonist," because she's the girl who can create her own narrative, rather than relying on someone else to do it for her. And in the world of the play (as in my earlier play *The Triple Happiness*), narrating one's own story is the key to survival. My (all-male) writers' group doesn't see this. The first time I bring pages in, I am told to "cut the best friend. She's not as interesting as the hot mean girl."

Again it is true that a stable (and gorgeous, light-filled) home, a financial cushion, and the right roommate have helped me to feel grounded and happy. This is an idyllic time, one of the best yet. Life at the Princess Apartment is easy and joyful. I get up early and either write or head over to Jivamukti for morning Vinyasa practice, then down to the magazine where I work as research editor, a nice euphemism for fact-checker. I work until six or seven and then meet Emma for theater or drinks or dinner or all of the above. Occasionally, I still see Noah, but Emma insists he's probably not The One. She makes fun of the way we fight ("I can't talk to you. I can't talk to you. I can't even talk to you because you won't even listen!"), but she respects the place he clearly still holds in my heart. As a fellow lover of the Victorian novel, I can explain it to her best through Emily Brontë: "He's always, always in my mind—not as a pleasure, any more than I am always a pleasure to myself, but as my own being." Which doesn't stop either Noah or me from seeing other people. But how can you "cheat on" your own being? And referencing another English writer, I can say, Virginia Woolf was right—a set income and a room of my own yield results. I write three full-length plays and a handful of shorts during the year and a half of living here. I even try my hand at YA fiction. I spread out, relax, feel my feet on the ground—and grow. A lot.

In the spring of 2001, Marilyn makes her final visit to New York City to see my play *The Triple Happiness,* which is being "workshopped" by the Hourglass Group, a small but vibrant downtown theater company. She and Ida spend the weekend at the luxury hotel across the street from the Princess Apartment. I am proud to show her where I live and how well it's all turned out. "Look, Mom," I can say. "SoHo!"

Marilyn understands SoHo. She understands lofts and boutique shopping. She understands the Cupping Room, where we used to eat when I was a Barnard student and we visited galleries and downtown coffeehouses. This is the last of my apartments that she will see. In retrospect, I'm glad it was somewhere fashionable. There are the usual tantrums. (She can't wait in a line for a table during the Sunday brunch rush. "Do you know who I am?" she demands. The hostess at the Paris Commune could care less.) But there are also the usual exclamations of love, tears, affection, pride—and the sadness that pervades everything I do after she leaves. So I go to yoga and therapy; I meditate and take walks and drink water, waiting for the clouds to pass. As they always do.

A few months later, I am invited to workshop *Smashing* at the Eugene O'Neill Theater Center in Waterford, Connecticut. The O'Neill is set up to be a "conference" in which playwrights develop their plays with directors and actors—but the focus is as much on exchange and dialogue with one another as on the plays we're developing. The writers are in residence for roughly a month, and that summer, by chance, most of the eight playwrights are in our early thirties, and we quickly become friends. Rehearsals are "open," which means writers are invited to sit in and observe how other writer/director pairs work. There are late-night walks on the beach, confessions, love affairs, dramaturgy sessions, and new writing—it's summer camp for playwrights. When Emma visits, to see the production and spy on my latest (unavailable, deeply wrong for me) actor crush, she refers to herself as "my wife" so that we can get her free tickets to the show. "I'm the closest thing to a wife you've got," she says dryly.

I get home from the O'Neill in August and am immediately confronted by a delicious heat wave, a new boyfriend, and the absence of air-conditioning. Emma and I have prided ourselves on our French sensibilities, not needing or wanting AC. We live in such a big space, with open windows and cross-breezes—who needs it? But that August it's hot. And I can't sleep. This time, the insomnia has nothing to do with rape or PTSD and loneliness; instead, it's about hunger.

My days at the magazine are numbered. The work, besides being menial (okay, detail oriented), doesn't pay enough for the hours I put in, and now that the award money is gone, I can no longer afford to work part-time for $20 an hour. I want more. What I want, really, is to hold on to the luminous feeling of the past month at the O'Neill, the sense of community and the distinct experience of being treated like "a real artist." It was like arriving at the grown-ups' table after years of sitting with the kids in the other room. And I like the grown-ups.

I decide I need a bed when the new man discovers I sleep on a futon on the floor and remarks, "I suppose that could be adorable," in a tone that indicates he doesn't really think so. My friend Julia agrees, stating that in her opinion, "After you turn thirty, you have to sleep at least a foot off the ground." So I decide to elevate my life by elevating my sleeping arrangements. I think that raising myself off the literal and figurative floor will "raise" my expectations—and maybe, possibly, everything else in my life. Maybe this bed is like a "feng shui" rite to encourage expansion, upward-moving growth. When I ask Noah what he thinks, he—still sore that I'm seeing someone new, someone I actually *like*—shuts the whole thing down. "Just get a better futon, Girl," he says with disgust. And I think, Noah and I are not moving up together. He does not support my rise.

However, Marilyn does. She's thrilled to hear I want some material comfort (At last! I'm really her daughter!), and even offers to pay for it as an early birthday present. I haven't taken money from my mom in years, and I'd hate to regress, but there is something symbolic in allowing my mother to help in this endeavor, like a wedding registry for my imagined "new life." So at first I say no but then quickly change my mind. Besides, I'm basically out of cash after my year of "raising the bottom" and unsure how I will make ends meet come fall. My "cushion," the award money, enabled the part-time freelance magazine work. And that's gone. And Marilyn says she has some money from a recent PR job and she would like nothing more than to share it with me. It's a pleasure for her, she says, that she can afford to do so. I think maybe this is part of the symbolism of the thing, a gift from my mother, a mother's blessing. This blessing will help me to rise off the floor, receive my new lover—who is a proper grown-up, not an actor—and earn more than $20 an hour.

I hit Macy's. I have no idea how to buy a bed, so I buy clothes first. A red skirt, feminine and silky, like the kind Emma wears. And then a brown sweater for the fall. By the time I finally make it downstairs to the mattress department, I have no idea what I'm looking for. Soft? Firm? Pillow-top? Contour? What's the difference?

I enlist the help of my girlfriends, hitting all the major stores, investigating. I'm amused when Stella pushes down on the mattresses with her fists, trying them out, she says, "for sex." I mention that no sex I have ever had looks remotely like what she is doing to those mattresses, but what do I know? I slept on futons and fucked in vans with Noah. After a week of shopping, I select one, on my own, at Kleinsleep—and it's perfect. A full-size pillow-top with some kind of certified sleep-something. The bed arrives late one afternoon, and after helping the delivery guys get into the apartment, Emma and I go to Lucky Strike to celebrate my emergent adulthood. The only thing is, I don't actually want to sleep on it. I kind of just want to look at it. It is so perfect and unspoiled. I take the plastic off and stare at the thing like it's an alien. And that night I sleep on the couch. It takes me a full week before I can bring myself to sleep on my new bed. But once I do, there's no going back. Who knew such restful nights were possible? I wonder if my insomnia would have been cured years ago if only I'd had proper back support and a pillow-top?

When I tell Penney how gorgeous the O'Neill was, how I've finally arrived, found my place, and fallen in love, not to mention how I'm ready to take on the world, she smiles and says in her beautifully mysterious way, "Not yet."

"What do you mean, *not yet?* This is everything I've wanted, everything I've worked for! I'm finally happy! I have a home! My work is getting done! I met a man who doesn't live in a van! He even likes my work!"

She says, "It's not the time for that. Not yet."

"But—" I argue.

"I'm telling you," she says, "something's not right in the world . . . and it's all about to change again really soon—this isn't your real place yet. Nobody can find their place while the world is shifting so rapidly. Don't worry, sweetie. Just keep doing the work."

Two weeks later, I'm at my desk writing when Emma charges into my room speechless, pointing at something just

outside my window. Annoyed, I point out that I'm working. And I've told her numerous times not to interrupt me
when I'm trying to write. Ignoring my crankiness, she takes
me by the hand and leads me to the window until I see what
she's been trying to show me all along. We stand together,
watching, as the second building, the South Tower, which
has just been hit, disintegrates into silver dust. Silver dust!
Like a special-effects cue from those sci-fi movies I used to
see with Noah. Emma gasps. "This is the picture we'll see,"
she says. "This is what everyone will remember." We don't
own a television (just a monitor, which Emma has rigged so
that it will, under no circumstances, get any TV reception,
ever), so we turn on the radio and listen to NPR and watch
the street down below. People start running—straight up
our street from the Financial District—with white cloths
over their faces to protect them from the air, which smells
like burning things and death.

After spending the rest of the day inside and field-
ing calls (me to Noah: "Go up on your roof and look."
Grandma Ida to me: "Are you okay? This is just like Pearl
Harbor!"), I decide I can't stay inside any longer and go out
to buy groceries. Besides, it's scary. Friends keep calling to
say "Fill the bathtub with water" and "Get your flashlights
ready." *What flashlights?* At the store, a woman asks, "Are you
buying just what you need? Or stocking up?" I confess I
really don't know.

Later that night, Emma and I drink shots of whiskey
and go exploring. We play Girl Detective, winding through
the streets of TriBeCa trying to avoid the police and the
barricades to see how far we can get, dashing in and out of
doorways and through alleys, making our way south. The
air is full of smoke and ash. We get as far as Chambers Street

when the final blockades and television cameras stop us. A
reporter from a network news station thrusts a microphone
in my face, asking me how I feel and where I live—when I
tell her I live on West Broadway and Grand, she takes the
microphone away with some disappointment, saying, "We
want people who were really close to Ground Zero. People
being forced out of their homes. People whose pets are
locked up and can't get out, that sort of thing."

And then we can't breathe and can't get any closer, so we
just go home, wondering what will come next. The next few
days in lower Manhattan are like a science fiction movie,
right before or after the aliens come. There are National
Guardsmen with rifles at checkpoints on Houston Street
and then again on Canal. The mayor is urging people to
"shop" in an attempt to support New York's economy. But
our neighborhood is a ghost town. Unable to take the isolation or the smell, we get into Emma's car and drive to her
grandparents' house in New England, listening to NPR all
the way there. A few days later we return to the city, and as
soon as the neighborhood reopens, I return to work at the
magazine.

The rest of the fall goes by quietly and with dread. I'm
not afraid of another attack or of "anthrax on the subway"
like many of my coworkers. But the smell of death is everywhere, and I'm afraid of vague unknowable things. The
long-range effects of any of it—the attacks, the PTSD, the
potential environmental toxins in our neighborhood—are
wild cards. I hear FEMA is giving away air purifiers, but
we are just a few blocks too far to qualify. Noah calls to say,
"I was hanging out with the NYU kids in Union Square,
and I gotta tell you, I'm not a pacifist." One day, while
closing an issue at work, one of the interns bursts into a

campy ironic song and dance about looking for Osama (set to *Hair*'s "Donna"), and I think, I have got to get my shit out of here. This is not the time for irony. Or for declarations of love, as I'm told by the futon-hating boyfriend. He says, "Now is not the time," and I say, quoting a famous rabbi, "If not now, when?" And we break up.

The descent continues. My agent, a fellow music lover, takes me to a Bjork concert at Radio City Music Hall (the one where Bjork wears the famous swan dress and is backed up by a massive Icelandic girls choir) to cheer me up. (And it works. Bjork is heaven.) Afterward, I return the favor by taking my agent to a work party with an open bar. When we get downtown, to the chic Bowery Bar, home to many a *Sex and the City* episode, one of my coworkers informs me that there have been massive layoffs all day and that Sonya, the copy chief and my immediate supervisor, has gotten the ax. Sonya is hardworking and funny; she's often the person keeping it real at the magazine. I fight my way through the crowded club looking for her so that I can hear what's happened, and more important, how she's doing. But when I find Sonya and tell her how sorry I am, how much I'll miss working with her, etc., she says, "Well, you're fired, too. They told me to tell you." And I return to my agent, who is holding court at the open bar, and inform her, "I just got laid off." We leave the party immediately, heading for Cosmopolitans and refuge at a place called Angel's Share.

As a part-time freelancer (thirty-five hours a week, three weeks a month), I am ineligible for unemployment benefits. I have less than $1,000 in the bank and no prospects for future earnings. The award money is long gone—it lasted a full year (and with the last $1,000, before

taxes and the O'Neill, I went to a yoga ashram on Paradise
Island in the Bahamas—because what else are you going to
do with the final installment of a gift from God?). I start a
full-time all-encompassing search for work. The first step
is assembling a "teaching résumé" and then a "clips package" because I have realized that I want to do both. I miss
November rent—which Emma sanctions—and, looking for
any income I can create, start teaching a "creative writing
workshop" in the loft. I charge $300 for an eight-week
class and, with the six students I get, am able to just afford
December rent, groceries, and office supplies for my job
hunt. I send query letters and my "clips package" to magazines like the one that's just laid me off. I stalk MediaBistro,
a Web site catering to freelance writer types. My playwriting endeavors are working out all right—I have a workshop
of *Smashing* lined up and a production of two one-act plays
(for which I will earn a grand total of $3,000)—but every-
thing else feels like it's falling apart fast. Can it get any
worse?

In fact, it can. And it does. I spend a miserable New
Year's Eve by myself at the yoga center and then in my room
trying to drink myself into oblivion, which doesn't really
work because I can't have more than two drinks without
falling asleep. The next day I make resolutions—but I
don't know what to resolve, besides *stop being a moving target*.
Less than two weeks later, Emma is diagnosed with cancer.
We've been fighting lately—more than usual—but she is still,
in my mind at least, a sister. The night she gets her diagnosis, she and her college friends go for expensive cocktails
at the Soho Grand—and then she comes home and tells
me the news. The doctors think it's leukemia; they want

her in the hospital the next morning. Tests are conducted. Chemo begins. She doesn't come home. That night, I head uptown to the hospital, bringing Emma enough clothes and a few books and promising my loyalty.

I run into Noah on lower Broadway the night that Emma is admitted to the hospital. He's been taking classes in the neighborhood, but still it's unusual to see each other like this. I tell him what has happened and where my roommate is now. He frowns. "I don't trust the medical establishment," he says, offering to cook macrobiotic food for her, should she want, and to hold me, should I want. Which I do. Noah starts coming around again, and I start to imagine that maybe now, after all of these years, we'll finally get it right. One thing about Noah—he's loyal. And we still love each other. I think, *Maybe it was him all along. Maybe we had to travel this far to earn each other. Maybe this is how we choose love.* Emma doesn't appreciate it when I bring Noah to the hospital to consult with her about detoxifying through macrobiotics, but I need him.

At this point, I'm a mess. Eight years earlier, with Sam, I could show up, sit in the hospital every day, and give unconditionally. I was barely supporting myself then, but I was twenty-four and in love with my best friend, and the world was transforming faster than I could keep up with; all that mattered was light. This is different. For one thing, I have to work. It is no longer permissible to barely support myself. Since getting laid off ("let go") from the magazine, I've been looking for both steady jobs and also new ways of making money—ideally through freelance writing or a teaching career. I've been sending pitches and queries and "clips" to downtown magazines like *Interview* and *Nylon* while setting up interviews with theaters that have strong education programs. This takes a lot of time. And then, there's my writing, without which I am lost. But also I have become more "real"—grounded, hopefully—and less in the clouds. Although I was obsessed with Sam's predicament, the truth is, Emma means more to me. She's tangible, a day-to-day relationship, someone I rely on and share a home with. I find it impossible to detach. Her illness and dramatic relocation to the oncology ward have me scared and upset and definitely regressing. The whole thing reminds me of my mom. And I'm unfortunately transparent. I've always been that way—what I think and feel is all over my face, usually on my lips as well. Plus, there are all of these anxious and sometimes intrusive phone calls from Emma's mother, who is (obviously and appropriately) panicked. ("Brooke, can you bring Emma's TV to the hospital? Can you find Emma's obscure book of German poetry? Brooke, Emma needs her mail . . ." and so forth.) The worst part is, the woman's tone has the opposite of its intended effect—it makes me want to protect my time and energy and prioritize the job hunt that I can't afford to put on hold instead of dropping everything for her daughter, my friend.

Exhausted, upset, guilty, and never a hearty lover of winter, I come down with a cold about a week into Emma's hospital stay. A cold means I can't visit. I have germs. I am contagious. The oncology ward requires pristine hygiene so that the chemo patients, whose immune systems are being torn down piece by piece in order to kill the cancer, won't get sicker. Emma and I talk on the phone every day, more than once. But I keep my distance during the germ phase. I am grateful for the break, which I see as an opportunity to take care of my own careening emotions. Unfortunately, I'm honest about it with Emma. What a mistake.

I find out about Emma's plan for my relocation from a

mutual friend the night before my next hospital visit. I've been away just less than a week, healing the cold, taking massive amounts of echinacea and vitamin C, sleeping, and drinking water. But like I said, we're talking on the phone. So I am shocked when I run into a mutual friend who says, "That's so generous. What you're doing for Emma." I ask with some confusion, "What am I doing for her?" Blushing, this girl describes the arrangements that Emma has made, involving my temporary move out of the loft. I haven't heard anything about it. Like I've said, I've been imagining that I'm a part of the family, a member of the home team. I've been thinking that once we get through this initial circus, I will be most helpful by keeping it real in the apartment, making her laugh, treating her like my friend Emma rather than "Emma with Cancer." We've even been joking about hats and wigs. But now I realize I've gotten it all wrong.

I want to talk to her immediately but the phone lines are shut down at night, and she's probably asleep. I leave a long, desperate message on her voice mail, furious that she's made a plan for both my living situation and work space without discussing it with me. Why can't I have some say over where I go? Which means, here I am venting my anger on the voice mail of the sick girl. Shit.

When we finally speak, the next morning, Emma admits that it's a rash and possibly extreme plan, but she wants me to move out and make room for her friend/ex-boyfriend, who will move in. She says, "You're one of the most generous people I know. But you give in ways that are good for you. And right now, I need someone who can give in ways that are good for me." She says, "I have to be selfish." Who can argue with that?

At this point, I have no money saved, no job, and no

plans. No relatives in New York City that I can turn to. No boyfriend to "crash with." (Noah either doesn't offer or isn't empowered to do so based on his own sketchy living situation.) Thus, I have no idea what I'm going to do. I do know that I won't go live in Emma's ex-boyfriend's apartment, as they have both suggested. I can't handle a share with two strangers (his roommates) during such a tumultuous time, especially when I'm sending out letters, putting together résumés, and looking for work. It is of note that Emma's mother's apartment will lie vacant for the next few months while she also moves in to our place to take care of her daughter, but no one will offer me temporary respite there, or any money to help me get situated elsewhere. Nor will I ask. No one will admit—until Emma does, years later—that they've put me in an impossible position.

"She has cancer, Brooke," says one of Emma's writers in a matter-of-fact tone, as if that should answer everything. But the girl who says it lives rent free in an apartment her parents bought for her and works part-time at NYU as an amusement, not out of real necessity, so what does she know about needing a place to live or having to find one without any kind of savings or help! For that matter, what does she know about cancer?

I've developed (a strange and sometimes unfortunate) immunity to extreme circumstances over the years. I don't know if it's my own history with rape and Sam's mental illness or years of processing my mother's health troubles, but to me "She has cancer, Brooke" might also mean "She's healing herself through a miraculous and brave process that looks like a disease." It might mean "She's the newest heroine on a superhero TV show, only she's slaying aberrant cells instead of demons—and really, aren't they the same?" I imagine that the "sick" person wants to be treated as honestly as possible, with a sense of humor (like Sam always had), and without kid gloves. And that includes sharing my feelings with her, in the hopes that she'll share hers. But in the words of my 9/11 beau, "now is not the time" for my feelings or Buffy the Vampire Slayer jokes. Neither are what Emma, or her family, wants.

Emma insists that I am not being banished and that it's not forever. She promises that I can "come home" as soon as this first phase is over, and so I pack my favorite things, as if going away for two months. This is our initial deal. Two months while she gets resettled after the hospital and goes through her first outpatient treatments—of which she's unquestionably scared—and then, she insists, I can come "home" and we'll make the next set of decisions together. I leave everything else—dishes, business and creative files, my printer, and my mail—at the loft. And I head uptown, one big suitcase and a laptop in tow.

....

250 West 103rd Street

My friend Monica has arranged for me to stay in her boyfriend's place while he's out of town. Monica's boyfriend is also a friend of mine, but all communication about the apartment and/or my situation there will pass through her, including the two days when he will be in New York and I'll have to vacate, heading for an air mattress in Brooklyn. (I request permission for the velvet couch at "home" in the loft, but permission is denied.)

Monica's boyfriend's apartment is just thirteen blocks

from my first Barnard dorm room, and thus I feel I've been
sent back to the beginning of my NYC tenure to take stock.
It is an awkward homecoming. I have never been so miserable or so disoriented, at least not since the summer of
1993. I wonder if there's an astrological component, like a
Pluto transit, because it feels like the Infinite Universe just
took out an ax and swung.

The apartment itself is bright and friendly—orange
walls, blue trim, a warm kitchen stocked with spices and
peanut butter. There are more books than I have ever seen
in one domestic space—they cover the bookshelves in double rows and are packed into the closets and kitchen cabi-
nets. I decide to read as many of them as I possibly can in
the coming months. If I'm going to be homeless, I might
as well get an education. I start with Proust but soon give
him up for Haruki Murakami, who seems to get my mood—
abandonment, imprecise loss, and a little bit of wonder.

I go back into therapy, and my new therapist says, "This
is amazing! In all of New York City, you found the one
person to live with who would reenact your deepest childhood wound!" I wish he looked less thrilled with the whole
thing. I'm a fan of psychological breakthroughs, but this is
ridiculous. Yes, yes, I'm healing. Yes, yes, this is probably
good. But it hurts like a motherfucker. I have lost everything I counted on. I have no money, no apartment, no
job, and no love once Noah dumps me for a Sarah Lawrence student whom he's been intermittently seeing (without my knowledge) for weeks because, as he says, "I thought
you were fucking some other guy." (I wasn't.)

"When in my miserable, homeless, therapy-fueled,
oncology-visiting life would I have had time to do that?"
I demand.

He says, "Maybe I was just afraid of it happening later."
And then he admits that he really likes this girl ("She's
already important to me.") and needs to be free to pursue a new relationship. It's a horrible but basically loving
conversation—at least it's honest—and when we get off the
phone I wrap myself in a blanket because there is a chill
inside, and I can't seem to get warm. I feel like Cordelia in
King Lear, the good daughter who, by virtue of her refusal to
play up to her father, is excommunicated from the family
and sent away, banished. I have been banished to 103rd
Street. I'd have preferred, like the real Cordelia, to go to
France.

Meanwhile, most of my clothes and all of my books, files,
and dishes—not to mention my desk, the armchair from
Park Slope, and the bed—are still in the loft, in my old
room, where I imagine my replacement, the ex-boyfriend,
using them. Emma has agreed to let me continue to teach
my Wednesday night writing workshop for the next few
weeks, while she's in the hospital—but when I go back there,
I'm a visitor. I feel like I should sign in and wear a badge
like I used to in the psych ward with Sam. Only what rela-
tion would I state? Former tenant? Former sister? Former
friend? Renovations are under way in the loft as Emma's
parents have decided to take this moment to cover the
exposed brick and create a more efficient kitchen. In their
defense, I'm sure they need an outlet, a project with more
reliable and immediate results than recovering from cancer,
which is mysterious and slow going. But it certainly adds
to the chaos. Especially when they put another of Emma's
former roommates in charge of the project, and he is the
one granting me access to my own files, desk, closet, and
mail.

Most mornings, after making coffee and oatmeal at the
apartment, I walk to the Cathedral of St. John the Divine,
sit in the gardens, and weep. I know, it's dramatic, but
it helps. I am starting all over again, right back at square
one. I have never felt more alone. What I can't see at the
time, but I can see now, is that this is when the light gets
in. As Penney points out, I am growing at a ridiculous rate,
shedding things—beliefs, relationships, and identities. I
am shedding everything that no longer fits. If only I could
release more and judge the pain less.

One morning, I decide to treat myself to a $7 manicure
on upper Broadway. It's a treat, but I need a treat. And I
can spare $7. Okay, I can just spare $7. But it helps me feel
taken care of, and it's a worthwhile indulgence. At least
until later that night, at dinner with my friend Josh, when
I reach for my wallet and realize . . . it's gone.

Josh says, "Don't worry. I'm sure it's in your other bag."
And he gets the check. But once home, I realize that my wallet isn't in another bag, or a pocket, or anywhere. I retrace
my steps and then call the "missing and stolen" debit card
emergency number. I learn that someone has been charging phone cards and electronics all afternoon on my card—
and it isn't me. I cancel the card and at daybreak file a police
report. I am without cash, without ID, without my Social
Security card—and without my apartment.

And then, in an unexpected turn, I decide not to feel
sorry for myself. To take this stolen wallet in stride. To trust.
I decide to ignore the voice that says, *Everything you touch turns*
bad. Everything good will be thwarted. Everything you start to rely on or trust
will abandon you. Instead, I decide this is a test of courage and
faith. If I can proceed without fear, I'll get what I need. And
so, I walk the 107 blocks to the loft that night, from 103rd

to Broome, to teach my class. The walk takes all day, but I have all day. I stop whenever I need to, at one point using my new gym membership (which, in an unprecedented move toward debt, I am charging to the Visa card I've only just gotten) to catch a shower and steam at a crucial chilly midpoint. I'm encouraged by the knowledge that this is how I can take care of myself without asking for help. That night in my workshop, a student hands me $20 that she allegedly "owes" me (I'd forgotten) and I think, It's all going to be okay. And I take the subway home.

These are temporary victories in an otherwise bleak landscape. And it is bleak. Emma and I are barely speaking. She admits, in a horrible phone conversation in late February, that I'll have to look for a new place to live, that the "temporary" is "permanent"—and that I will have to arrange with her ex-boyfriend/new roommate exactly how and when I gain entry to pack my things because "he's exhausted and needs some time" in my—I mean, her—apartment. "I have to be selfish now," she repeats.

I wake up on the morning of my thirty-third birthday more miserable than I have felt in years—reminding myself that I'm homeless. Jane, an Irish lighting designer with a birthday close to mine, explains that it's my "Jesus year" and thus everything is meant to fall apart so that I can wander the desert, find my true calling, and be crucified and resurrected. I wish the crucifixion part would hurry the fuck up and hurt less.

I meet Illiam, a beautiful Puerto Rican filmmaker, at a dinner party in Jackson Heights. We have an immediate connection, and I find myself telling her my story, as one is wont to do with a stranger at a dinner party in Jackson Heights. "I'm miserable without a home," I tell her, "ungrounded, depressed, at sea.... Barely getting out of bed in the mornings."

Her response? "Pretend you're on tour." She says, "If you were a musician or an actor touring with a show, you'd be living out of a suitcase like you are now, but from hotel to hotel, every few weeks or months—and you'd have to figure out how to make yourself at home in each new place very quickly so that you could get on with the business of doing your work." And isn't this the key? Aren't I meant to be doing my work? Doesn't this sound a lot like what my first therapist used to say, eleven years ago, about getting out of limbo? Illiam is a messenger from the smart world. She says, "This is your chance to build a new skill. You have to learn to make yourself at home wherever you are." She suggests identifying a few things that will give me a sense of belonging and comfort—beauty, even—quickly. And making a kit. Which reminds me of an e-mail that a playwright friend once sent me with his teacher's rules for working out of town. The wise teacher urged her students to get a lot of rest when out of town and make every hotel room into a "home" by bringing a candle in a tin and taping a picture or two to the generic walls. A home kit!

The next day, following her advice, I buy myself a vanilla-grapefruit scented candle, which I set on the kitchen table next to a photograph of golden yellow leaves that Penney shot in Central Park (she's been selling pictures with healing properties for the last year or two, and clearly I could use whatever help I can get right now). I set up an altar with sage, some rocks I've been holding on to since that time in Vermont, a shell or two from my trip to the Bahamas, and images of "home."

Penney sends me to see a tarot reader as a birthday

gift—my sole present besides the flowers from my friends in Louisville and the bed my mom bought me six months earlier. I haul my ass down to Brooklyn Heights, to an apartment uncomfortably near to where I lived with Bryan the summer I was raped. The neighborhood itself, the lovely promenade and tree-lined streets near the water, remind me how I used to feel that July, when I wanted to "heal" but didn't know how to enact a healing. When I wanted a home, but didn't know how to create or attach to one. And now, here I am again, with the very same questions.

"What's wrong with you?" asks the Buddhist tarot reader. "You look sick."

"My roommate has cancer."

"But you don't have cancer."

"No. I don't."

"Because," she says, "you look sick."

Thanks a lot.

But she continues, "You need some sun. You look like you're internalizing her illness. You think if you get sick, too, it'll make her better. . . . And you don't yet realize that you deserve to have your basic needs taken care of. Just because she's sick, it doesn't mean you have to suffer. It certainly doesn't mean that you can't have a home."

That's a lot of information. She goes on, "The two of you are each on a journey, and now your paths diverge . . . you'll be apart from one another." All this in the first ten minutes of an hourlong reading. She's good.

She says, "What line of work are you in? Because this, here"—she holds up a card—"is the prostitution card."

"I'm a playwright."

"Well, it looks like you work in the sex industry."

I shake my head no, but she insists I must be prostituting

myself in other ways. And all I can think of is Emma and that gorgeous loft. And how I have made us "family" in order to keep living there. How I have, in fact, tied my fortunes to other people repeatedly, and given my love in exchange for more tangible things. Why do I still live with a roommate, anyway? Economics aside, why aren't I entirely self-supporting? Which is when I realize that I've made a grave, grave mistake. I expected someone else—Emma or her family, who are not my family—to take care of me. And, like the Canadian girl who didn't want me to leave my boxes in her apartment after I was no longer paying rent, or Wes, who had to put my things in storage when the friend I'd gotten to sublet my room moved out so abruptly, it isn't anyone else's responsibility—ever—to do so.

The tarot reader says, "You deserve to have a place to live. You can have that...even when someone else is suffering. Her suffering is not yours." And it's as if a light has been turned on and all of the bad thoughts, the self-inflicting-doom thoughts, the ones about my life falling apart or, worse yet, being taken from me in sacrifice, start to dissipate. Light reaches every corner of my mind, of my thinking. *It's not personal.* Emma's sickness isn't about me. I don't have to keep myself in pain in order to liberate her. *I deserve to be happy.*

I leave the tarot reader's apartment and start walking across the Brooklyn Bridge, on a path above water, no solid ground. Now what? I imagine Scarlett O'Hara clutching "the red earth of Tara" and saying, "As God is my witness, I'll never be hungry again." So as I walk, I tell myself: With the Infinite Universe and the East River of Manhattan as my witnesses, I will never be homeless again. I will earn enough money to take care of myself. I will create stability.

And in making this vow, refusing to suffer on behalf of someone else's suffering, standing up for my most basic need—a home—something good starts kicking in.

I apply for—and get—a modest sum of money from the September 11th Fund. *Paper* magazine's layoffs were entirely related to their loss of advertising money after the attacks (once TriBeCa was quarantined, people were less likely to spend money at the Odeon, which was then less likely to take out big ads in *Paper*). I also apply for emergency funds from both PEN and the Dramatists Guild, writers' organizations to which I belong. And these, too, I receive. I can't look for a new place to live until I can save some money. And I can't save money until I can get some more work. But I have to pay rent—and now a lone credit card bill—in the meantime. So I work at finding work.

I arrange with Emma to get into the loft and pack up my things, and I use some of the emergency fund money to rent a storage space and hire a mover who takes all day and who seems to think "efficiency" means one box at a time in the elevator. (How hard can it be? We have an elevator!)

While packing—a process that takes a week and involves going into the loft while Emma and her mom are out of town—I decide to jettison anything I don't totally love and need, which means I give away a third of my belongings. And it feels amazing. Mostly, during this week, I stay uptown, but the night before the mover arrives, I stay in the loft, with plans to sleep on that beloved velvet couch (where I tearfully watched so many episodes of *Felicity* on our disabled monitor with the VHS option, thinking, My love life will work out just as soon as hers does). But I don't sleep that night. And not because of insomnia. I'm awake with the clarity of the all-nighter, the buzz I used to get in

college the night before a paper was due, sorting through
old photographs and letters. I'm sitting in the enormous
closet, because it has its own small discrete light source,
filling entire garbage bags with reminders of the past. I
think, *I am the person who had these experiences. I don't need to keep the
artifacts.* I think of the way food digests—you take it inside
of you, you break it down, it becomes a part of your body
(and energy), and then you let it go. Why not do the same
with objects, pictures, letters? Suddenly, I'm able to throw
away things that I had been holding on to for years. I don't
want to be reminded of the past. I want to let go. I want to
move forward.

The Man with Van arrives in the morning confused and
calling from the corner. ("I see 340 and 350, but not 345,"
he says, forgetting that all the odd-numbered buildings are
directly across the street from the even-numbered ones.
Or maybe he's just high. It's hard to say.) It takes all day
to move into Chelsea Mini-Storage, even with my reduced
lot. I do most of the work and buy the confused—and now
slightly creepy—mover a slice of pizza when the work is done.
(Over pizza—his pepperoni and mine mushroom—he says,
"Hitler was a vegetarian, too, you know.")

I have my mail transferred from the loft to my agent's
office. And now I'm officially adrift. On a life raft called
103rd Street in a very big river. Except that I will have to
leave 103rd Street, too. Soon. But this does not frighten
me. I have located some kind of strength. Maybe it is Penney or the prayer and meditation and daily sage-smudging
or the enormous pots of vegetarian soup I'm cooking to
save money. Or maybe it's just time. Or maybe it's me. But
the aforementioned "something good" is fueling my days
and informing my next set of actions.

By the first of March, I am teaching in two different arts programs through MCC Theater and running a free after-school master class for NYC public high school students. But more on that in a minute. The main thing is, by mid-March I will have enough money for a sublet. And my friend Dee knows of just the thing.

....

*Address Unknown, 28th Street
and 35th Avenue, Queens*

This is the only place in which I've lived that I will entirely forget the address. Many years later, I will again live in this neighborhood, moving in with my boyfriend (now fiancé), and walk by the buildings, unable to identify which one I lived in. Clearly, it was a traumatizing experience.

I'm subletting from Phil, who is subletting from Steve, who is subletting from someone else who really lives here— and they are all out of town for months. I share the place with Tim, an actor and accordion player, who dates Dee, who is my friend. The best part about the entire experience is that I now see Dee a few times a week. And Tim seems to want to be the big brother I never had, or at least the straight big brother I discovered I had after my gay brother Wes left home. We take turns making coffee in the mornings, which we both like strong, and he waits for me to come home at night, keeping an eye on me, making sure I am safe. I look forward to our mornings over coffee or our late nights— over ice cream—dissecting the day. Tim is another of these radical guardian angels sent to me in times of need.

I have two jobs, which keep me working four days a

week. On Wednesday afternoons, I teach playwriting to members of the MCC Youth Company, a free after-school program geared toward giving NYC public high school students rigorous training in the professional theater. To this day, these are some of my favorite teaching experiences and some of my most talented students. These young playwrights teach me how to teach. I meet with them weekly for four years—Josh, Nicole, John, Holland, Kyle, Valini, Veralyn, Devonne, Maya—and as they grow up, so do I.

I am also teaching three days a week at Unity, an alternative public school that has been set up for kids who have failed out of every other school they've gone to. In the initial meeting, the principal refers to her student body as "dead-end kids." But they're hardly dead-end. These kids have more life than I've seen in some time. They're fierce and angry and verbal—which makes for gorgeous writing. Scenes, plays, and poems—they tell it like it is. These students are hands down the best thing to come into my world, and I love them fiercely. From the armed security guard (a woman!) to the overworked teachers to the neglectful and financially strained system, these kids are constantly put to the test. But then, lately, so am I. We're a good match. And if they're distrustful of the girl who comes traipsing into their classroom wearing red bell-bottoms and secondhand vanilla-colored cowboy boots, annoyed that, as one kid, Christian, says, "No offense, Miss, but we didn't ask for this shit—creative writing don't help us pass the Regents Exam," the fact is, they have every right to be distrustful.

Little by little, I earn their trust and respect. I keep coming back. Plus, I have a genuine passion for what I teach, and I tell them the truth. I say: Write what you want (except for swear words, which their principal doesn't allow). Speak up. Put your feelings into words. Don't stop writing. I invent exercises like "Write about your grandma's hands" and "Write a letter to a famous person." I make them write plays in which characters fight to get their needs met, but I don't let them resort to the clichés of guns and violence. "If a character has a gun," I say, "you're cheating. Because I know who has the power in the scene. The person with the gun doesn't have to work to get their needs met, they just shoot." The rule in our classroom is no guns and no rape. Because, as I tell them, I know a little about the latter and have a deep distrust of the former. I bring in pieces of writing—from my own play *Dancing with a Devil* (It's about the rape. It's chilling when, after we read it, a quiet girl says to me privately, "That happened to my friend. Can I give her this play?") to Adam Rapp's *Nocturne* to Allen Ginsberg's poem about Walt Whitman in the supermarket in California ("Damn, he angry," says a tall girl with ponytails). I bring them to see *Topdog Underdog* on Broadway that spring (the sight of Mos Def without his shirt on is great incentive to be nice to the teacher who brought them there). "There are black people in this play!" the kids say, impressed and with some disbelief. "Yes!" I say, happy to correct the notion that plays aren't written about anyone who looks like them. I will teach here on and off for the next two years, in what feels like a perfect meeting of hungry creative minds. And God has a sense of humor: the school is located two blocks away from Emma's loft. I'm home again. As a day worker.

By April my life settles into a routine. I teach three days a week in Manhattan. The other four, I try to stay in Queens and not spend money. It's challenging since there's no hipster café, no movie theater I can walk to, no real center for young artists—my neighbors are older or married with kids. So I find myself going into Manhattan whenever possible, trying to slip back into my old life. Sometimes I bring my laptop and write, as I've finally started a new play, *Sam and Lucy*. The play begins as an inquiry into romantic love, but ultimately evolves into a story about a daughter's ability to finally let go of her mother, who has recently died. The germinating seeds of the play have come from my O'Neill boyfriend, who said, "I can tell by knowing you that your parents were in love."

To which I replied, "They were divorced by the time I was four. But yes . . . they were most certainly in love. Weren't yours?"

"No," he said. "Still married. But never in love."

This conversation has haunted me. The more I think about it, the more convinced I am that the stories we are told govern what we believe possible. Marilyn taught me that true love is possible, and I still believe it. Maddy, the mother in *Sam and Lucy*, dies in the final scenes of the play and because of this, I never let Marilyn finish reading it. As much as she loves seeing herself in print, this one is too close to home.

Another gift of the spring of 2002, a new love interest! Alex is a composer with a background in dance and martial arts, a kind of jack-of-all-trades artist. He has gotten my number from the sound designer I made out with a few years earlier. We meet in the Greek cafés along Broadway, in Astoria. Alex asks me to write the text for a music project of his and although I try to refuse ("I'm not working for free"), it's no use. He's too damn cute. Tall, blond, like a fairy tale, a skinny Prince Charming in oversized thrift shop suits. While working together, composing text and music, we start to kiss. When I complain about my sublet, Alex invites me to move into his apartment. It seems he has to be out of town for a few weeks and would like nothing more than to imagine me living there rent free as compensation for my work.

Despite Tim, I've been miserable in the Queens sublet. Most mornings, when I head outside, I'm disoriented to see lawns and families—I miss the boutiques, celebrities, and bars of lower SoHo. Plus, when I go out at night—part of the job description when you work in the theater (rehearsals, performances, friends' shows, drinks, and shoptalk)—cabs become necessary, as the walk from the nearly deserted subway after I A.M. is sketchy. I'm blowing money right and left while trying to save for my own place.

Alex's apartment is also in Queens, but it's closer to the neighborhood where young actors and dancers are living—Astoria. There is a brick-oven pizza place and a fairly decent French bakery in walking distance, not to mention baklava. And who doesn't love a good piece of baklava? And staying here, even for a few weeks, seems like a way of getting closer to something that I value, something I need and want, even if I can't name what that thing might be. Or maybe I just have a crush.

I move into his place for a three-week stay. But the best news is, by the beginning of May I have enough money saved to start looking for my own apartment, which I plan to do just as soon as I unpack. And return Alex's calls.

....

33rd Street and 30th Avenue, Queens

Alex has a great apartment. With an air conditioner. And although we've only just kissed a few times—okay, we fully made out in the middle of a park under bright stars and again on Elizabeth Street under bright streetlights—I feel that he might be The One. Penney's been saying, "Someone is coming. It isn't anyone you already know, and it isn't Noah." But whoever this new man is, "He's so good you hardly believe he's real." In addition, she says, the new man has been going through some kind of "health crisis" that has changed and made him ready for someone like me. She says I can't go looking for him—this one will find me. Which reminds me of that great Marianne Williamson quote, "Do not seek for love but seek instead all the barriers you hold against love's coming."

Still, I've been collecting evidence that Alex might be "The Guy." For one thing, he had knee surgery a few years ago—so that's the health crisis. Also, he is the sole caretaker for a sick parent, doing the very thing I have neglected to do for my mother, which is, make his father's illness his main priority. So yes, he's so good I don't believe he's real. Or else, maybe he's codependent. But mostly, it's the light in his pale blue eyes—a deliberate reference to Lou Reed—and our shared love of the Velvet Underground and obscure West German postmodern dance that makes me think, This guy is special.

Alex's apartment is painted like a Moroccan café. The kitchen is the color of sunflowers. And his sheets are—oh my God—so soft that it feels like special genetically engineered silkworms wove them while dreaming of sugarplums. My own bed is wrapped in plastic and stored in the West Chelsea storage facility, and I hadn't been sleeping too well on the foldout sofa bed at 103rd Street or the overly precious queen-size whatever in the 28th Street sublet. This bed, as Goldilocks might say, feels just right. How did

I get here? I wonder, savoring it, savoring him, or at least my fantasy of him. And where am I? And how long will it last? I think, *Maybe this is how people find their home.* And when I call him from his apartment to convey messages about mail or the answering machine or to ask for a good dry cleaner, his cell phone lights up with the word "home." He answers, "Hello, Home," and I melt. I have never been someone's home before. Not even Noah's. We start talking on the phone at the end of our respective days. He reads poetry to me—*Prufrock*—and I tell him about my adventures looking for an apartment in a neighborhood "so uptown, it's downtown."

Yes! I'm looking at apartments! Because although I'm slightly delusional regarding Alex ("looking to get rescued by a man," says Penney, wisely), I'm not totally out of it. As much as I'm fantasizing that this is "The Guy" (which means I can move in), I have also been looking at studio apartments in Washington Heights and Inwood, the two neighborhoods at the very northern tip of the island of Manhattan. I'm considering taking a studio for $900 a month when I receive an onslaught of good news. First, my play *Until We Find Each Other* has been accepted at the O'Neill, which means another residency in Connecticut, and then the same play will go to Steppenwolf Theatre in Chicago for a full production. This means that I'll be out of town for the entire month of July and half of August—six weeks. I will return to New York for the month of September, then leave again, for Chicago, for the play's rehearsal period, culminating in an opening night on November 4. In addition, I've just been accepted into a seven-year residency program at New Dramatists, a national organization founded

in 1949 by Michaela O'Harra to support the work of playwrights. And more good news: Job-hunting pursuits from
as far back as January are starting to pay off. I am offered
a well-paid freelance position for the month of June at
one of the Condé Nast magazines—*House & Garden*. No joke.
(Which means, despite God's weird sense of humor when
it comes to titles, *income*.) After an eight-month period
in which I felt cursed, this wave of blessings is welcome
indeed.

I'm always amazed when, after a period of struggle and
loss, goodness follows. It's the most natural thing—the
Universe moves one way and then, to balance itself, it moves
in the other direction. But I'm amazed anyhow. When
things are bad, I'm afraid that they will be bad forever, and
when they're good, I'm ridiculous enough to believe the
goodness will last. This is exactly why people become Buddhist.

But I am also amazed by the courage that it takes to receive
a blessing. My limitations are safe. When I'm struggling, I
know what to do and who to be: I don't spend money. I eat
what I can afford, walk everywhere, and refrain from making purchases of any kind. When I have money, I am forced
to make choices, to stand up for what I want, to speak up, to
clarify. I find that with abundance comes a kind of sobriety,
in which we must admit that none of it is personal. Loss
isn't personal. And neither are blessings. We don't succeed
because we are inherently good and worthy (or thinking the
right thoughts, using the right language, making the right
collages) just as we don't suffer because we're inherently
flawed. Both fortune and loss come to us, visit for a time,
and leave. It is all, as the Buddhists say, impersonal passing

phenomena. And right now, after experiencing both sides, in such short order, this has never felt truer.

I make a strange choice. With a little money saved and out-of-town work on the horizon, I decide, Why not keep saving? Why take a $900 apartment that I'm going to have to sublet while I leave town for two months, come home for three weeks, and then leave again? I finally have the resources to pursue a rental, but it's not yet the right time. So with the faith I've been gathering, I follow my gut and float . . . just a little bit longer.

I look for temporary shelter. Fortunately, New Dramatists has a few monastic dorm rooms reserved for members who find themselves in a crunch or out-of-town members fleeing their home communities for the inspiration, joy, and networking potential of New York City. I need one month—June—while I work at Condé Nast and prepare for the O'Neill. And it just so happens one month is the limit that a writer can "crash." I'm in luck! A plan! I tell Alex that I have somewhere to go when he returns, but again he urges me to stay as long as I want.

I tell him I will stay through the end of May. And then Alex calls to let me know that he's coming home a few days early.

"Should I go?" I ask.

"No, no," he assures me. "I'm looking forward to sharing space with you."

"You have one bed," I say, reminding him that sharing space is the same thing as sharing a bed. There is no response.

Which leaves me giddy, already anticipating . . .

On the night of Alex's return, I am babysitting on the

Upper West Side of Manhattan and reverting back to high
school behavior, killing time to avoid going "home." After
work, I head for Barnes & Noble, loitering in the magazine section. I check movie times. I call friends. No one
is around, and no distractions are available. Finally I'm
forced to ask myself, What's up? Why am I so resistant? He
said I'm welcome! He said he wants me there! So I break
it down. On the one hand, I already feel like I "belong
to him," or at least with him, by the simple fact of sleeping in his bed and taking in his mail. And I have a massive crush. On the other hand, this reluctance could be
because I already know the whole thing is make-believe and
thus flawed. But how, I ask, will I find that out unless I try?
Eventually, I will have to go home. Why not now, when he's
still awake?

I hail a cab. "Astoria, please."

When I arrive, Alex is in the bathtub, a martini shaker
in the freezer, glasses chilling, and classical music playing.
I catch my breath. It's like a romantic movie. I call a shaky
"hello" into the bathroom but head in the other direction, for
the living room, where I take off my coat and boots and sit on
the carpeting wondering, Now what? Am I supposed to join
him in that tub? Should I slip into something more comfortable? What might that something be? But before I can
take any ridiculous fantasy-based action, Alex is out of the
bathtub and making his way over to me, on his floor. And
it's all so good, I don't know what to do. I start to cry, thinking, Maybe, just maybe, this is my happy ending. Maybe this
is how people find their home. (Crying on someone's floor
in Astoria? Really?)

There are so many times I have asked the question: *Am*

I home? With each apartment, each group of friends, each new life phase: *Maybe this is how people find their home.* I can't yet see that the situations all carry impermanence because, like most of life, it's an impermanent conversation. The answer will keep shifting so long as I place home outside myself. But for now, I do not have that insight, just a desire for Alex and his pale blue eyes.

His bathrobe comes off, along with my dress, as he takes me into his bedroom, which has for the last two weeks been mine. And despite the actor I kissed at Monica's birthday party (the one who pointed at assorted places on my face and neck, saying, "I'm going to kiss you there," just before he did), this is the first time I've attempted to be physically intimate since—well, since Noah the week before he dumped me for the Sarah Lawrence student. I've missed touch. And it's all beautiful—until, completely naked, Alex says, "You're going to love my girlfriend. I really can't wait until you meet her." And I sit up in bed shocked. *"What!? What do you mean, GIRLFRIEND?"*

He sits up too, admitting that, yes, he did just use that word. No, he hadn't planned on it sounding like an ménage à trois or a foreign movie—he just thought we'd get along. The girlfriend, it seems, is a ballroom dance instructor he met through the aikido dojo, and Alex has nothing kinky in mind when he says we'll meet. He wants to keep seeing me. And he says that while he's not "in love," he is in a healthy and supportive relationship—that he has no intention of ending—with her.

"What were you thinking?" I ask.

"It's an open relationship," he offers.

I get out of bed, desperately looking for something to wrap around my naked body.

"Well, I can't stay here."

He looks surprised, which makes me angry. "Did you really think I'd just *stay* here!"

He stammers. He hadn't thought about it. But why not? Yes, he admits. He thought I could just stay here. Maybe it's all that postmodern structure-less music he likes. He imagines that so many permutations of "relationship" are possible. Maybe I led him on, reading all that Milan Kundera in his bed. Maybe, like Sabina, he's looking for some form of erotic friendship. But not me. I may be unconventional, but I'm also a nice Jewish girl from the suburbs (at least when it's convenient), and I can't do this.

I rush to put my clothes on and pack my things—and I'm out of there, in a car service, immediately.

Where do you go in the middle of the night when the guy you thought you were moving in with confesses he has a girlfriend?

One of my closest friends, a beautiful actress named Yvonne, is house-sitting on the Lower East Side. "Of course you can come here," she says when I explain the situation from the car. I arrive twenty minutes later with my stuff, and she sets me up on the futon in the living room.

"What was he *thinking*?" she asks with a shudder.

"He says it's an open relationship."

"Does his girlfriend know that?"

Later I whine to Penney, "I really liked him!"

She'll have none of it. "No, you didn't," she says. "He was a port in the storm." She scolds, "You have to stop trying to get rescued by a man."

"What are you talking about? I'm not trying to get rescued!"

But she's right. Why was I staying in his apartment, without paying rent, pretending he was my boyfriend?

Yvonne says, "Give yourself a break. It's been a rough year. And everyone wants to be rescued now and then." She herself is staying in a friend's apartment, having given up her room in a Williamsburg loft after the environmental toxicity got to her. She's saving money, like me, and dreaming of her own place. We're two peas in a proverbial pod, and I wonder, *How long does it take?*

part four

Getting It. At Last.

Summer 2002—The Present

424 West 44th Street
The Eugene O'Neill Theater Center,
Waterford, CT
The Days Inn, Chicago, IL
205 West 103rd Street

After Memorial Day weekend, I put my now-portable self into a cab and head for New Dramatists, which is housed in an old church in Hell's Kitchen. The building screams *history*. It has enormous wooden doors, vaulted ceilings, stained-glass windows, and, now that it also houses playwrights, a packed liquor cabinet. On the main floor, there are the offices, a library and sitting area, and a "black box" studio theater. On the second floor there are more offices, a kitchen, a "writing nook," and a big theater with enormous ceilings and proper theater chairs. One more flight up, there is yet another set of offices and a few basic dorm rooms that members refer to as "Seventh Heaven." Rumor has it that August Wilson wrote *Joe Turner's Come and Gone* when he was staying in these rooms. Rumor also has it that he had some gorgeous love affairs. (And I listen to rumors.) Numerous other playwright-members have stayed in Seventh Heaven, never for very long, with the one exception of one Pulitzer Prize winner who, before his award, famously lived in a room next to the lighting booth on and off for years. And it's entirely free for current resident playwrights. Did I mention that part?

On my first night in the church, I set up the "Home Kit."
I tack a photograph, taken by Penney, of Central Park leaves
across the wall and hang a vintage slip over the window as
a makeshift window dressing. I take my grapefruit-vanilla
candle out for decoration if not actual usage, as no candles
are permitted in Seventh Heaven. It's eerie to spend the
night entirely alone in such an enormous building—but it's
a holy place. And when I can't sleep, I listen to the sounds
of the street below. And they soothe rather than frighten
me. In the morning, I wake up alone (with sunlight and
a lot of quiet) and head downstairs to the industrial-sized
coffee machine, doing a line of pirouettes, in my pajamas,
across the theater floor as I go.

Later that afternoon, I'm sitting on the front steps
of the building savoring the temporary respite when my
grandmother calls with disturbing news. Marilyn has been
rushed to the hospital, unconscious. I don't know how
to respond. Years of dealing with my mom's dramatic
phone calls ("Well, the paramedics were here again last
night") have trained me to not panic immediately. Years
of very good therapy have taught me to take a breath and
wait a beat before freaking out in response to reports of
each crisis. The news is always frightening, but Marilyn always survives. However, that might not be the case
today. For one thing, it's not her on the phone. My sweet
mother is in the intensive care unit—which Ida refers to
as "ICU," making it sound just a little like DKNY. Marilyn's doctors, whom I insist upon speaking to, say, "You
should be here. This might be your last chance to see her
alive." Still calm, though steadily becoming less so, I book
a flight.

My mother's death is the thing I have been most afraid

of my entire life, apart from getting raped, and that already happened. Honestly, though, the fear of Marilyn's death is more threatening to me, and more primal, than anything, including the rape. Since childhood, it's the game I play with myself in the middle of the night when I can't sleep: What if this means my mother has died? Or, when I was a little girl and she was late to pick me up from school: What if this means she's gotten into a car accident, or gone into diabetic shock somewhere, and she's gone? Moreover, without my mother, who will love me? Since her first stay in the hospital—in the seventies, when she became diabetic—these are the thoughts that have run through my head on a regular basis. All therapy has been geared toward relieving me not only of the terror but also the belief that her health (both physical and emotional) is my responsibility. (Years of fights in which she'd yell, "Stress is the worst possible thing for my diabetes, and you give me stress!" or the winner, "You're angry at me for being sick." I'd counter her with "No, Mom, I think you're angry at yourself and projecting.") Today, in June 2002, after months of coping with transience and a hospitalized roommate who is now a stranger, I'm susceptible to psychic holdover. Terrified, I wonder, *Is this it?* Despite the difficulty of our relationship and the familiar fights we have, Marilyn is my only parent, and sometimes it still feels like her and me against the world.

When I arrive in Detroit the next morning, I head straight for the hospital where tiny, frail Marilyn is unconscious and hooked up to a variety of machines. The doctors explain that they don't know if the root of the problem is her heart, her lungs, or her kidneys—all of which have stopped working. They say, "Her entire system is compromised."

The diabetes has been wreaking havoc on her body, aging her organs and making her vulnerable to attack. They say, "Your mother is a fighter, but she's fragile." I take a tiny rock, blessed by Penney, and tape it to the side of her hospital bed. I am hoping that this will reach where the medical establishment can't. Because truly, not one of the doctors has a cohesive analysis of the problem or a plan to raise my mom from the dead. The heart doctors say it's her heart, the lung doctors say it's her lungs, the kidney doctors say it's her kidneys . . . and one doctor even says, "We don't know what to do for her."

I want to be with her, next to her, touching her. She looks smaller in that hospital bed, tiny and vulnerable. I hold her hand and stroke her face. No one touches sick people. And Marilyn loves to be touched. Later, after she recovers, she'll say that she remembers seeing me when I came into her room, that she opened her eyes, and I looked like a stack of colored plastic doughnuts, like the children's toy, with each round, brightly colored piece stacked upon the next, and at the top, my messy ponytail and a lot of light— the kind I myself used to see. She will say, "I knew how much you loved me, and I wanted to tell you that I loved you, too, but I couldn't get myself to speak. . . . I'd just have to close my eyes again." And perhaps that is what it was like.

When I leave the hospital, I drive back to her condominium in a nearby suburb, sometimes stopping at T.J. Maxx to roam up and down the aisles, just like my mom used to do, trying to unwind. And then I sit in her apartment, working on my play. I feel very, very lonely. I write e-mails to her each night, telling her what the hospital was like that day, what she did or didn't do, what I did or didn't do, who I saw (her friend Rosemary), what I thought about (her boyfriends and her music), and mostly how much I love her and want her to get better. Although she does get better, she never reads these e-mails. By the time Marilyn is back at home and using her computer, she's completely forgotten her password and all things associated with her e-mail account. And even when she hires someone to create new accounts and new passwords, she never recovers the information or the record I left for her of that week in June.

I head back to New York—Marilyn is still unconscious, and in ICU—to start my monthlong fact-checking job at *House & Garden*. Ida promises to keep her eye on my mom, and keep me up to date on what's happening. If I have to come back, I will. But we're both hoping that Marilyn will recover. And in the meantime, I still have to show up for work. I cry through the entire flight home, sure my mom is dying, unable to take my eyes off the lights in the sky, wondering if this rupturing, shaky feeling will be with me always.

I arrive dazed and start making calls. No one is around. And not sure what else to do or who might feel good to talk to in this moment (oh how I wish there were someone who'd feel good to talk to) I call Alex. He understands my situation all too well from taking care of his father. He is gentle and comforting. Especially when he offers to pick me up from the airport, a small miracle in New York City. For the most part, no one I know has a car, so no one ever just offers to pick me up. The only time I am ever picked up from the airport is in Detroit, by my mom or grandma. But Alex has a rental car, through some minor stroke of good fortune, and it's not due back until the next day. He offers. I accept.

When Alex arrives, we drive straight to the Plaza Hotel and charge a round of cocktails to my mother. I haven't used her credit cards in years (the last time was dramatic and involved running out of money in the UK and needing a hotel room and crucial theater tickets) but now, with her dying and all, it seems like an appropriate moment. I order a whiskey. Alex has a martini. And I tell him all about the week with my family. I tell him about trying to break into Marilyn's safe deposit box to see if she left a living will. I tell him about the lonely aisles of T.J. Maxx. I tell him what the doctor told me, "We really just don't know . . ." He understands. He listens. He takes my hand. When the bill comes, I use Marilyn's American Express card, and I mail the receipt to her, at her condominium, writing on the back, "By the time you get this, you're either dead, in which case it doesn't matter, or you've recovered, in which case you owe me a drink." And then beneath it, "I love you so much, and am praying for your recovery. At the Plaza with a tall, handsome man—I think you'd approve." And, of course, the joy of my mother is that when she did recover and did receive this bill, at her home address, she called to tell me that she absolutely did approve. But later that night, when Alex escorts me back to the church and takes me upstairs, we both remember the girlfriend—his— and I think, Do *I*?

The next day, I start work at *House & Garden*. There is the usual first-day banter: Who are you? Where do you live? What other things do you do besides work as a free-lancer for this magazine? My answers are ridiculous: I'm a writer. I don't live anywhere. Well, I'm living at a play-wrights' organization in Hell's Kitchen this month. And I have a play going up in a friend's apartment in Brooklyn in three weeks, and then I go to Connecticut and Chicago to workshop another play. It's a lot. My coworkers, in the windowless den where the fact-checkers are sequestered, are amazed by all this. They think I'm an oddity—but we enjoy one another. And I am at work when I get the first phone call assuring me that my mom is out of danger and in good spirits.

The best thing about this summer, in its strange, strange transience and strange, strange life-and-death tone, is that my friend Patch is directing a production of a play I wrote at Juilliard called—again, appropriately—*Playing House*. On the weekends, I join Patch and Yvonne and a bunch of Juilliard friends at Kimiye's loft, rehearsing the play and hanging out. When I'm working on a play, the rest of the world sorts itself out. And so, in this strange time, I find ease. I work at *House & Garden* during the week and live in the old church and go to Williamsburg to rehearse my play at night and on the weekends. Ever so briefly, I get involved again (and then quickly uninvolved) with Alex; of course, it ends badly, as does anything we pursue for the wrong reasons, out of lust and hunger and boredom. Our final breakup occurs at Bed Bath & Beyond on my lunch hour from work. I'm buying him a set of sheets (don't ask why) when Alex says, "Someday this will all be very funny." I respond, "Only if we're married." And then we stop seeing each other altogether.

In the last week of June, I pack up my things again. I take what I no longer need back to storage and carry the bag I'll live out of for the rest of the summer—along with my laptop and some almonds—to Penn Station, where I board a train for Connecticut and the familiarity of the O'Neill.

I spend a month in "my old room" at the O'Neill, with the pretty pale yellow walls, hoping that the familiarity will ground me. I talk to Marilyn every few days, which is more contact than we've had in some time. It's comforting to hear her voice after almost losing her. And, true to character, she's funny. When the hospital bills start coming, her response is incredulous. "They did a lot of tests," she says, amazed.

"Well, they thought you were dying," I say.

"Really? Why would they think that? Don't they know who I am?"

There are no love affairs for me this summer—just an awkward run-in with an ex who has moved on and an even more awkward exchange with an actor who wants to hook up. I am available for neither. I want whatever "settling" I can find after this tumultuous year—from the World Trade Center attacks to Emma's illness to my mother's illness to my own disappointments in work and love, now is *really* not the time.

Housing is, again, a pressing issue. A bunch of actors and playwrights sitting on the lawn one afternoon realize that at least five of us are between apartments and looking for our next home. Each has left his or her last situation and not yet found the next. Theater people used to be called "gypsies," and now I know why. We're all transient, composing a life through out-of-town jobs and temporary sublets.

"We should get a big house in Brooklyn together," someone says. But who has time to look for a big house in Brooklyn when all five of us are in Connecticut? All we can do is let go, wait, trust—and keep one another apprised of opportunity.

When the conference ends, I board a plane for Chicago and a residency at Steppenwolf, where I will be working to refine the play that they'll produce in November. The theater puts me up in a Days Inn on the North Side. I have my "Home Kit" ready. And now I really am on tour! I light a candle and make the room mine. In the evenings, after rehearsal and left to my own devices, I wander around the North Side of Chicago looking for the ghost of my high school self. I visit the bookstores and cafés I used to love. Some are still standing, but most have been turned into something else (a Starbucks, a Mexican restaurant). My high school self refuses to appear. I want to see someone I know or used to love, but most of my old friends have moved away. Still, I make weird, instinctual pilgrimages looking for clues. How did we grow up? Where is the girl I used to be when I spent whole afternoons drinking Earl Grey tea at Cafe Express and trying to avoid going home? The only clue I find is the absence of clues, which makes me realize I've moved on. It's like in a sci-fi movie: My frequency has changed. The past has no more business with me. And so I stop looking for the past.

I get back to New York in mid-August and have to work fast. I've arranged to go back to 103rd Street while Monica's boyfriend is again out of town. I have ten days to find my next sublet—which I do, miraculously, through a yoga teacher, whom I've e-mailed. And because of her,

I land back on my favorite block in all of Manhattan—a block I am now convinced holds some secret to my ability to begin anew.

....

428 East 9th Street

Troy is a novelist and yogi, and he's writing a book about the New York yoga scene. I write him a check for $1,000— less than his actual rent but the absolute most I can pay—for six weeks, during which time he'll go to Tuscany and I'll live in his apartment. Troy comes from a family of writers. Sitting at his desk and sleeping in his enormous (and expensive, he informs me) bed, I try to absorb their literary and spiritual legacy. I pretend that I might be one of them, the unrecognized sister of a pack of feral art children. I'm the one abandoned at birth and left with that family in the Midwest. Maybe someone lost me in a poker game. (No chance. I am most certainly the daughter of Marilyn and Harvey, the Holly Golightly and Jay Gatsby, or so I'm told, of the Jewish suburbs of Detroit.) But all I inherit from Troy is a small bug infestation, which I take care of by purging his pantry of old dry goods and spraying with toxic things he'll obviously disapprove of once he gets home.

Apart from the tiny mothlike insects, this is a sanctuary. I even sleep well. I'm relieved to be settled for six weeks on my favorite block in Manhattan, in such a beautiful space. Six weeks is luxurious. And I feel at home right away. I don't even need my kit. The apartment itself is a large 1BR with wooden floors and great light. The bold (but soft) colors make the place look like a yoga center or an artist's den. The walls are painted pale pale blue, and the shower curtain is deep red. The window curtains, which flutter when the wind sweeps through, are from the nearby Indian shops, and they're coral colored with little pieces of mirror and silver wound through. Troy has red and blue velvet floor cushions instead of chairs surrounding the exceptionally low dining room table, on which I eat all of my meals and even once give a massage to the cute actor who helped me move in.

Realizing that six weeks can go by very quickly, I get on the ball looking for a place to live. After seeing what's available, and how much it costs, I determine that I can't live alone and call Chernus, part of the "let's move to a house in Brooklyn" crew from July's O'Neill residency.

I've known Chernus since Juilliard, and to know Chernus is to love Chernus. It's Kismet that he needs a place at the exact same time I do. Although I had planned to live alone—and not with a twenty-five-year-old actor—Chernus just might be my best choice of roommate. He is intelligent, kind, certainly the funniest person I know—and patient with me. We share many of the same friends, similar life goals, similar values. And so with the help of Manhattan Apartments and the *Village Voice*, we start to look at shares. He wants Harlem; I want the East Village. We look at both. I win.

Working with a broker is an entirely new thing for me. Up until now, I've generally stayed away from them, finding my places through friends and word of mouth. But Chernus and I have a little bit of money saved, and we're on a time crunch. Plus, brokers are becoming more and more essential to Manhattan real estate. At one time I'd have said, *No way,* preferring to stalk the *Village Voice* (both in print and later online), walk around desired neighborhoods, knock on doors, establish contact directly with a management company or a super, even talk to local shop owners. But life in lower Manhattan (and Williamsburg and Greenpoint, for that matter) has changed (I blame the musical *Rent*). Apartments are scarce, and brokers have made themselves necessary. Chernus and I start with one uptown, who looks and sounds like Agent Smith from *The Matrix,* which freaks me out.

When I want to see an apartment being shown by another broker, I am torn. I ask, "Should we be loyal to Agent Smith?"

"Honey," says Chernus, as if speaking to a small, mentally challenged child, "they're brokers. We don't owe them anything."

Thus, with polygamous intent, we see other brokers, in other parts of town, telling each that he's the only one.

I use Troy's apartment as if it's an artists' retreat. I spend a lot of time alone, enjoying the silence. (And during the annual Charlie Parker Jazz Festival, one of my favorite reasons to be a New Yorker, I enjoy the saxophone, which reaches me at Troy's desk.) I slow down. This is the first time that I have been unemployed without simultaneously being desperate for cash. I still have money from the *House & Garden* job, but even better, another playwriting award, this time from the Berilla Kerr Foundation. So I can relax and spend my days writing and wandering, letting myself "fill up" again. I decide to do the opposite of what I did with award money two years earlier. Instead of "keeping the day job" and using the money as a "prudent

reserve," this time I live on the money, writing until it runs
out. It's an unusual and sometimes uncomfortable pleasure to have so much unstructured time. But I do not try to
fill it. Instead, I challenge myself to sit still. And when not
looking at apartments, I read Troy's cookbooks and make
big pots of harvest soup with vegetables from the Tompkins
Square farmers' market. I practice yoga. I write more for
pleasure than for a specific project, which means exploring,
journaling, taking notes but not trying to fit any of it into
a play. Instead, I indulge in the process, exploration for its
own sake. I wander the East Village, savoring my favorite
things about New York: sitting in cafés, reading in Tompkins Square Park, making daily visits to the vegan bakery on
St. Marks Place and the little espresso shop on Ninth. I eat
vegan food at the Life Café, window-shop in front of the
boutiques now lining blocks that were once full of squats.
I meet my friends in the evenings at St. Dymphna's, the
local Irish bar, and drink hard cider and flirt with boys. In
short, it's heaven.

Occasionally, on the weekends, I make pilgrimages to the
storage space in West Chelsea, where all of my things still
live. I sign in at the office and wear the sticker badge up in
the freight elevator, sometimes getting lost on the way to my
space. An extraordinary community of transients is here:
College kids, storing their things for the summer until they
can move into their next dorm rooms, mingle with weekend flea market vendors, who hold on to spaces in order to
store their wares. Musicians store instruments. People with
a lot of stuff and not a lot of closet space keep out-of-season
extras. I'm amazed at the community of it all! On my visits, I
unlock the space, ready to swap out a sweater for a sundress
or vice versa, and sometimes, out of nostalgia, I pull my big

upholstered chair into the hall and rest a moment, reading through a book or trying on one of my hats. And I wonder, how soon will I be able to claim my things?

Walking back to the bus, heading east to Troy's, I tell myself, *I am light. I hold on to nothing.* I'm like a caterpillar in some chrysalis process waiting for form. No shape, no structure—I have dissolved and liquefied. But the thing about holding on to nothing is that it can only last if you're a Buddhist monk, and even then, I think, you need some stuff. Eventually, I will have to hold on to something. Or choose to. And maybe, I think, it's what we choose to hold on to that creates meaning. If I open my arms wide, release what I'm holding, drop attachment and identification, I tell myself, whatever sticks is truly mine.

In September I'm inducted into New Dramatists at a formal ceremony. When the interns ask how many tickets I need for the event, I draw a blank. There is no one. Yvonne is out of town, Noah and I aren't speaking, Emma and I aren't speaking, Stella and I are—temporarily—not speaking, and I'm not dating. On the family side, my mom is too sick to travel, and my grandma takes care of my mom. In another few months, Chernus will become my de facto opening night and ceremony date, but we haven't yet crossed that threshold. And that means no one will come to this ceremony. I will have to find a way to enjoy it on my own.

Late that night, after the event and party, I climb into Troy's enormous bed feeling more lonely than proud of myself. The *Harry Potter* movie is on TV—Troy has some crazy digital cable—and I've never seen it. I realize that something is wrong when Harry Potter reduces me to tears; it is his invitation to Hogwarts that starts the floodgates. New

Dramatists is like Hogwarts, a mystery school where I will be initiated into my magic, trained to be effective, and given refuge—in Harry's case, from the sadistic aunt and uncle who continue to persecute him, and in my case . . . just the big bad world, life, financial pressure, and heartbreak. And in the middle of the night, in Troy's bed, at the end of the movie, with my first bout of insomnia in months—I do the strangest thing. I call Troy in Tuscany, hoping, on the off chance, that he'll talk to me and make the loneliness go away. Immediately I realize that this is not the case. He answers, concerned, "Umm . . . hi. Is everything okay in New York?" Playing it off, I make up some official (but not urgent, lest he worry) "house" reason for the call. The little bugs are back, and I'm throwing away his brown rice (which looks like it's been sitting there, in the glass mason jars, since the beginning of time). And I want to clear up some issues about the date I'm leaving, bullshit bullshit bullshit. He is so deeply uninterested in talking to me about any of this. Quickly, I end the call and get off the phone, facing my loneliness head-on. So what if there's no one to share blessings with? So what if my family can't understand my life or be here? Was their approval *ever* something I courted? Honestly, no. I ask myself, Can I be satisfied—and grateful for just this very peace? The accomplishments have been for myself, not for my family or Noah, or the dream of future love. Can I befriend this exquisite loneliness? Because, while painful, it also feels sweet, as if the loneliness itself could open and prepare me to become more present, more compassionate, even more comfortable. I think of how often I hear myself saying "I'm alone" or "There's no one," and the thing is, it's a lie. Despite the lack of family members

in attendance at an awards ceremony, despite being single
and on the outs with one or two friends, the truth is, I am
blessed to be part of a vibrant community, I have a lot of
friends, and I've never really been alone. And I had better get a handle on how I describe myself and my situation
ASAP. That night, I vow to use different language and to
acknowledge, however and wherever I can, the number of
blessings in my life, the people who love me, and the absolute abundance of it. And to breathe through any moment
when the lie of isolation starts to seduce me into feeling
otherwise.

A few days later, on Rosh Hashanah, the Jewish New
Year, I sit in Tompkins Square Park thinking about the
nature of these hard-won and bittersweet victories. No one
said we wouldn't be alone at times. No one promised we'd
get our hands held as we faced the challenges. And challenges were, in fact, promised. I remember now when I was
a kid and people would say, "A life in the theater? That's
really hard." And, arrogantly, I'd think, It won't be hard
for me. But now I understand that it's really, objectively
hard—for everyone. I work in a profession in which there
is no clear path, no "right way" to go, and no reward for
growth. Instead, there are a surplus of worthy plays and
writers (and actors and directors and designers) and a defi-
cit of opportunities to produce them. And once a writer
is produced, he or she faces still more deficits in budget
and stability. Even though I've been getting produced—
in great theaters across the United States; I've even been
flown to London for residencies and workshops—I still need
other jobs to support myself. Would I give up this life in order
to do something else? Absolutely not. This is what I want,

it's all I've ever wanted. And if it's true that the only reward
for growth is the growth itself, this is good! Very, very good!
What else, besides the growth, matters? And then I think,
My entire life—at this very moment—is a blessing. It is the life I asked
for years ago, when I stared out the window at the Regency
Hotel thinking, I could belong to this. I have done just what
I set out to do and fought the very dragons that stymied my
mother. No wonder our relationship has been fraught! I
was fighting for both of us. And the freer I can become,
the more actualized, the more good I will do on her behalf
as well. We will both be liberated. In fact, years from now,
before my mother dies, in our very last conversation, she
will say to me, "I want you to know I understand every choice
you made, and I'm proud of you. You did what I couldn't."

....

200 East 7th Street

"What if you guys live here forever?" asks our friend Fay as
we unpack the U-Haul on moving day.

I look at her, panic-stricken, wanting to heave. I love
Chernus—indeed, he will become one of my most trusted
and important friends—but living with a platonic male
roommate seven years younger than myself in a small
two-bedroom fifth-floor walk-up "forever" is just not sustainable. I mean, right? The lessons of the past year have
not been leading up to "forever" in a walk-up with a roommate, even if it is a roommate I like and in my favorite
neighborhood. Have they? I cry actual tears at the thought
of "forever" here—even more intensely when I see the

black plastic TV stand and night tables waiting on the curb below. After the year and a half in Emma's West Broadway Princess Apartment and another nine months of drifting, I was really hoping for a substantial adult home without plastic furniture. And while Seventh Street will be a home in many, many ways, it's not the one I'd fantasized about. I've put my dream of a small, private, adult Virginia Woolfian space on hold in order to stay in lower Manhattan and keep my expenses under control. It's a sensible move, one I never once regret, but when Fay says "forever" I feel some momentary disorientation. And then I get over it, take a breath, and deal.

Our moving crew—mostly Juilliard actors and friends—resembles the cast of a CW show. (Let's call it "The EV," for East Village.) I bribe one of the overly coiffed handsome actors with a steak dinner if he can prevent anything composed of black plastic from entering my new home, which he does. And Chernus and I have our first fight when he learns of it. "What's so awful about my furniture?" he demands.

When he unpacks my dishes, he understands.

"Shit," he says. "These are real. I feel like we're in Vermont or something."

We strike a compromise. Black plastic in his bedroom. Antique wood in mine. Shared aesthetics in the common space.

We have found our new home through the friend of a friend who volunteers in the community gardens on Avenue B and also works at a nearby real estate agency. Mary Beth, our broker, is a singer who moonlights (daylights?) for the company that manages this apartment building, and they happen to have a vacancy. The day I see it—impulsively, after meeting Mary Beth in the gardens—I know we have to move here. I call Chernus, who rushes in from Park Slope to see the place, and after some discussion, he agrees—this will be our home. Plus, I agree to let him have the bigger bedroom.

Unpacking is a joy. I open every box that first day, thrilled to see my things again—clothes, books, files. They have been far from me, in storage, since moving out of Emma's some nine months earlier. And the transformative process, aka the cocoon, has done its work. As I unpack, I realize how little of my stuff I actually need or want. The idea of missing my stuff was greater than the stuff itself. Okay, there are those "Vermont" dishes—mostly mugs and a few brightly colored bowls I bought in Mexico a few years earlier. But again, just as during the packing process, unpacking leads to shedding. I donate bags full of books to Housing Works and leave clothes I no longer want on the doorstep of the mission, just a few doors west. I only keep what will fit into this remarkably small space. And it's just enough.

My bedroom is roughly the size of the closet at Emma's. My bed, freshly revived from its storage phase, takes up most of the available space. The dresser just barely fits, and once I buy a tiny child-size antique desk, the room is full. But it's exactly the kind of space I want right now. I keep thinking of an Ntozake Shange poem, a favorite of mine, called "Where the Heart Is." She writes about living in a house like a small castle.

Where I can love myself in an empty
Space / & maybe fill it with kisses.

This tiny sweet bedroom on East Seventh Street reminds me of *that*. I vow to love myself here. And maybe, maybe, fill the room with—somebody else's—kisses.

Immediately, I leave town to start rehearsals in Chicago. I'm gone for three weeks—sleeping in the guest room of a friend from high school while working on the play every day and every night. It's ironic that now I have a home, but I'm not in it. Chernus leaves sweet messages—he bought a shower curtain and hopes I'll like it, he bought bookshelves, he likes some tiny Tibetan sculpture he's glimpsed in my room ("Luging Buddha," he calls it). But I am in Chicago to work, and so I focus on the play.

During a first production of a new play, it is common for the writer to be present—revising, editing, and working with the director and actors, and sometimes designers, to make the thing work "off the page." This is the period in which the play ceases to be mine and instead starts belonging to the actors who will inhabit and live inside of it each night. There is some irony here as I realize that my job is to create a world that other people can live inside of—without me. It feels like my housing: entering a space, making it my own, and then leaving it to someone else's care. Leaving an imprint, then moving on. The play opens November 4, and the next day I am back in New York City, ready to shop.

Armed with a list of things we need—a sofa, kitchen chairs, bathroom organizers—we make a date to visit IKEA. Chernus's new girlfriend has a car and, moreover, a side business as a professional organizer. A Virgo, she knows how to get things done—how to make a list, check it twice, and get out of IKEA in an hour. But after following us through the superstore as I look at and touch *everything* while Chernus cracks jokes about Swedish fish, she gives up and heads for the café. Watching her go, Chernus points at a display area where brightly colored furniture is arranged as if in some fictional character's home and says, "Who would I be if I were that guy?" Pointing out that there are bunk beds and beanbags, I say, "You'd be twelve."

Finally, though, we get what we need. Once home, we proudly refer to our design concept as "Nouveau Sesame Street," since it's all about primary colors and glee. One afternoon, I find a bald mannequin head on St. Marks Place and bring her home to add to the decor. "Don t bring that thing into my house," says Chernus. "What if it has chlamydia?" He puts a wool hat on her bald head and christens her Chlamydia Jones, giving her a perch on the windowsill, where she is our mascot and patron saint. Nouveau Sesame Street meets East Village trash-rehab. You could almost imagine Kermit the Frog or Elmo appearing in our brightly colored apartment to sing an impromptu song late at night. Chernus helps one imagine this because he is wont to sing improvisational songs of his own late at night. Like the ode to his ex-girlfriend's table: "I got her table," he croons. "I used to have the woman, but now I've got the table."

Life with Chernus is a make-believe sitcom. We call it "Between B and C," referencing both our initials and the two avenues we live between. I wish there were a word to adequately describe who he is to me during these years, but there is none. We look out for each other. We're invested in each other's lives and moreover—and in some ways even more valuable—each other's theatrical work. We share a value system based on creativity and laughter. He understands how my plays are put together and why, which is like understanding how I'm put together and why. And I think he's a comic genius, able to do the most amazing things, many of them in rhyme. Sometimes, late at night, drunk on a little whiskey, I'll say, "You're my domestic partner." But it's not really that either because, as he is wont to remind me when we hook up with our respective lovers, "We're not married." What we have is too good to be turned into anything else; the entire relationship falls under some Aquarian concept, a word that hasn't been invented yet, a new kind of family. I still want to use that word, even though I am starting to understand that saying "family" unleashes a series of expectations. And . I will get hurt.

But for now, I'm having a blast. Every night someone we know is in a play somewhere, which means there are drinks to be had, gatherings with playwrights and actors, and lively conversation. And it's always fun. Having been raised by intense women, I'd gravitated toward intense women; my best friends were girls, or else gay men. Now, suddenly, I find myself the lone platonic female in a circle of straight boys, Wendy in Neverland. These friends (and they're not new friends, I've known them for years, but suddenly they're the inner circle) teach me the silent solidarity of male friendship, a code of brotherhood. Unlike female best friends, the boys don't merge identities or try to borrow my clothes. Closeness isn't based on sameness. These boys keep their boundaries, their shape, in a way that girls, myself included, generally don't. They are brothers—loyal, protective, and dear. One look from me, in a bar or club, and one of them is instantly by my side "cock-blocking." ("Brookie, that guy has a girlfriend—let's go.") Most of my girlfriends are now in relationships or, worse, trying to persuade their commitment-phobic partners to straighten up and marry them. I want to talk about theater, about WORK;

my girlfriends want to talk about breeding. The boys offer refuge. We stay up late in bars laughing about *everything:* art, theater, philosophy, indie rock, and sex.

One night, I run into Noah and his new girlfriend a few blocks away from my apartment—which is, to my great dismay, also a few blocks away from *their* apartment. We catch each other's eye, and then stop in the middle of the block, staring. It's the first time we have seen each other since the last time we slept together. (On a night when Emma was in the hospital and, distracted, I left my laptop in a taxicab. Noah persuaded me that if we had sex it would act "as a Tantric ritual" to bring the computer back to me. And we did. And he was right. Anyway.) The Sarah Lawrence student, aka his girlfriend, clutches his hand and looks at me with a question mark. Determined to be gracious, I summon up some kind of hybrid "Carrie Bradshaw meets Grace Kelly" set of manners and ask, "How are you guys?" making overt eye contact with Sarah Lawrence, as if to say, I'm friendly. She looks back at me as if she knows more than she should, which makes me unfriendly. Mercifully, it's over soon and I head for the bar on Eleventh Street to tell Chernus all about the horrors of proximity and let someone buy me a drink.

A few days later Noah calls.

"That was weird," he says.

He asks how I've been and also, what I've been eating. And I'm standing in front of Commodities, the health food store, when he calls, and so I can give him a full account of both. We haven't spoken in months. He has missed my exodus from Emma's, both Queens apartments, my mom's health crisis, and my own adventures in Chicago. And I've missed him. But I don't say as much. We both get off the phone feeling, I imagine, uneasy.

A few months after *that,* Noah calls to tell me he's still in love with me.

He says, "I'm in love with you; I'm not in love with her. Why don't I come over right now? We can have sex, and I'll leave her and move in."

"Bad idea," I say. "For one thing, Chernus doesn't want to live with you." But really, I explain, Noah would only feel guilty and then start cheating on me with Sarah Lawrence. "Eventually, you'd want to go back to this girl who was 'already important' less than a year ago." And everybody would be upset.

"How do you like living with her?" I ask, cautiously, like treading on a minefield. Because the one thing I'd wanted, before we broke up in 1998, was to move in together.

"It's great," he says. And my heart sinks. Even more so when he continues, "I'm really happy," and then the line I will remember for years to come, "I'm still in love with you—but I don't think I could be with you every day."

A few weeks later, he calls to tell me that he and his girlfriend are moving to Seventh Street, just three buildings away from me and Chernus. She's already found the place.

"You can't live here," I say.

"Too late," he says.

"Tell her that I live on that block. And that you can't live three doors away from me."

"She doesn't care," he says with bravado.

"She should care," I say, reminding him that he's just declared his love for me and offered to leave her.

But he won't listen. The day they move in, I bring a guy home and kiss him on Noah's doorstep. Just to mark my territory.

Soon after that, we run into each other on the corner

and find ourselves making out in the back of the deli on Avenue B. We're both on our way to work, and after the kissing subsides, we walk to the subway on First Avenue, holding hands like we used to when we were in love. The whole thing is so strange. The bond between us has not been broken. And when we start meeting like this, Sarah Lawrence starts caring. Just as I said she should.

I don't want to be Noah's booty-call now that I'm not his girlfriend. And I don't want to be adulterous. But I call him when I purchase my first-ever air conditioner in the summer of 2003, asking, "Is there some kind of grandfather clause for ex-girlfriends that would allow you to come over and install my AC?"

Getting back together isn't even on the table. Nor do I think I want that. There's something healthier about the way Noah and I interact now that we're not boyfriend and girlfriend. For one thing, we're impeccably honest with each other. For another, none of our respective defense mechanisms are engaged. I don't cling. I don't need to. He is no longer the center of my world. And he doesn't evade. We meet when we want to meet. We're not trying to *get* anything we can't have. I think, It's very European, like in *The Unbearable Lightness of Being.* I was Tereza with Alex, but now I'm Sabina with Noah. And I think, Fuck that girl he lives with. Let her pick up his socks and pay his bills. I have what I want—his heart.

But a few days later, I watch them together from across the street—they're in the distance, near Tompkins Square, and I feel sick and sad and guilty. I leave him the message: "Don't cheat on your girlfriend." Which means her and not me. And later that same week Noah leaves us both, moving to a macrobiotic wife-swapping commune in Alaska (where he has been threatening to relocate since I met him nine years earlier), where he will stay for several months, making tofu and missing home.

If love on Seventh Street is less than ideal, work is perfect. I'm always at my most creative and prolific when I have a stable place to live and this phase is no exception. By the first of the year, I've started *Hunting and Gathering*. The play comes out of a writing exercise that I've thought up for the Unity kids. It goes something like this. I ask the students to each name something they're "an expert" in. No answer is too ridiculous. For instance, when one boy says he's an expert at being late to class, I incite him to write a detailed account of exactly how he manages this. (And there is, as I'd guessed, an elaborate system involved.) The second step, once they've identified an area of expertise, is to write a monologue in which a character with the same skill set teaches the audience how to do this thing. As an example, I read a list of all the apartments in which I have lived in the past fifteen years and claim my area of expertise as "finding an affordable place to live—and moving there."

I live this way, writing and teaching, until the money runs out. One night, I run into Emma at a party. She's with a group of her friends, and when we see each other, I shut down entirely. Truth be told, I'm regrettably cold. I turn away. I may even leave. But half an hour later, with painfully mixed emotions, I call her cell phone. That very night, we meet in a French-named American bar in my neighborhood where we sit down together and have the honest heart-to-heart we couldn't have had when she was still sick. Emma has been in full remission, thriving actually. Her tests are good, and she's excited about her life and her future. She's even in love. It feels great to see

her and great to get everything off our proverbial chests
and into dialogue. We talk for hours. If I want something
to change from this conversation, I can't say what it is. I
guess I want us to be close again, but maybe I just want her
to know that whether we're close or not, she'll always be
important to me. And we both say things like that. And
then we go back to our lives, stopping occasionally to see
each other, have a glass of wine or a meal, catch up and
laugh. And I guess that's what matters. The fact that we, as
people, get involved, get inside, affect one another, and
keep our hearts open.

Another friend back from the past, is Stella—who is
recently single and looking for reasons to stay out late.
We joyfully reconnect and start going to plays and movies, late-night dance clubs, and downtown hipster bars. In
addition to the stream of plays I see with Chernus and my
platonic boyfriends, there are now art openings and dance
clubs for Stella and me to infiltrate. These are the *Sex and
the City* years, and the New York downtown nightlife is different, no longer grunge. Suddenly the Lower East Side is
overrun with girls in fashionista dresses and fake Manolos
looking for fancy cocktails. I myself have many fancy cocktails. And I have crushes and make-out sessions in bars
with actors and musicians. And I practice yoga religiously.
Yoga is my favorite thing besides writing and thrift shops.

When it's time to earn money again, I get scrappy, piec-
ing together an income from freelance work and teaching.
One semester, I get a job teaching playwriting to undergrads at Eugene Lang College, part of the New School for
Social Research (where I refrain from mentioning that
despite graduating from a prestigious graduate program,
I don't actually have a bachelor's degree myself). The next

semester, I'm invited to teach at the University of Rochester, a job that requires a weekly commute on JetBlue. I
head to the airport each Monday morning pretending that
I'm going somewhere exotic, and each Monday I'm slightly
disappointed when the plane touches down in cold, col-
orless Rochester. I also work at *House & Garden* from time
to time, fact-checking. But teaching is my primary source
of income. I will teach at Eugene Lang, the University of
Rochester, Unity High School, George Washington High
School, Discovery High School, labor union 1199, and
privately, renting space from New Dramatists, while keeping my Wednesday afternoon master class with the MCC
Youth Company, who are still my favorites.

"You can have whatever life you want," I tell the MCC
kids, "at a price. If I can be an artist, you can be an artist.
You can make your dreams come true, so long as you're
prepared to work really unbelievably hard and give some
things up. I have a great life, but it doesn't include a television set, a stable home, or health insurance." (I have health
insurance now, but I didn't for ten years, between graduate school and Gordon, the man I will eventually marry.)
The students teach me, too. On the day that I invent a
writing exercise for "exorcism"—explaining how I need to
exorcise my long-term on again/off again boyfriend, one
sixteen-year-old with long black hair and a nose ring says,
"It's okay to hold on, Brooke."

I try to tell myself good stories during this period, stories about hard work and survival, about enjoying the process, "living the dream," and loving the present. But just
as I've always feared, there still seems to be some invisible thread that connects my confidence and my mother's

health. Just as I start to relax and enjoy my life, Marilyn gets the flu. She sounds remote when we speak on the phone or, in her words, "out of it." Since her hospital stay in 2002, both my grandmother and I are overly sensitive to any sign that my mother might need medical care, but during this flu she has in February, she refuses to go to the hospital, which is fine. Until it isn't fine. And she winds up back in the ICU.

At first, it's for a few weeks. The flu subsides, but then, she has a blister on her foot that isn't responding to treatment, and the doctors want "to keep an eye on it." The antirejection medicine she has been taking since her last transplant keeps her immune system intentionally compromised so that her body won't reject the kidney. Plus, her diabetes agitates everything else, so sores take longer to heal, if they heal at all. After two weeks, Marilyn happily reports she will go home on my birthday. But instead of going home, she contracts one of those strange pneumonias that people with prolonged stays in hospitals seem to get, and she is stuck in limbo. The day I turn thirty-four, she is completely unconscious. It's the first time ever that my mom can't say, "Happy Birthday," and I miss her voice saying it. The day is painfully long. I spend most of it panicking and feeling like the world is turning upside down again, inside. The party I'd planned a week earlier is unbearable. I don't want to tell everyone in the room, "My mom's in the hospital again," so I tell a few close friends and fake my way through the rest. It is her second hospital stay in less than a year, and she doesn't seem to be making progress. Is there any progress, in fact, to make? When I start the now-usual cycle of responses to my mom's impending doom—more insomnia, more panic, dark circles both literally under my eyes and figuratively underscoring my thoughts—my friend Lucy persuades me to talk to Marilyn's doctors directly.

"Is my mom dying?" I ask the kidney doctor straight up, because when you've spent a solid week trying to get hold of someone, why not get to the point when he finally returns the call?

He says, "No. She's not dying." *Relief.* "But we want to amputate her foot."

At the word "amputate" my throat closes; I am unable to speak or swallow. Since becoming diabetic in 1971, my mother has been afraid of two things—blindness and amputation. And now it seems one of her biggest fears is coming to pass. Plus, there is vanity involved: Marilyn's tiny feet ("It's too bad you have Grandma Rose's feet and not mine," she would say. "I have the nicest feet"), not to mention the nicest collection of designer shoes. Imelda Marcos had nothing on Marilyn Lucas Berman. Walter Steiger, Chanel, Charles Jourdan . . . these names were like *Sesame Street* characters to me. Kitten heels, ankle boots, stilettos. No more.

She says, "Don't come yet—it's a three-ring circus. Come when I'm back at home, when I'm in physical therapy. That's when I'll need you."

By the time she's made up her mind to amputate, some kind of superhuman strength has come to my mother and indeed, when I finally visit, a few weeks later, for Mother's Day, she has her manicurist there, at the hospital, making sure that the foot she still has is in good shape—and well appointed with sassy polish. Marilyn, meanwhile, is on the phone to Saks Fifth Avenue, ordering cosmetics.

When that's done, she calls a local Italian restaurant whose owner used to cut her hair, and she orders dinner (for my grandma to pick up) because, in her own words, "Hospital food sucks." We have a picnic meal that evening, over which she cries to me, "They're tearing me apart, limb by limb."

When I get back to New York I wander around in a daze. I work through the rest of the spring and summer—more teaching jobs, more fact-checking, a brief residency at the Williamstown Theatre Festival to work on my play *Smashing*, which will be produced in the fall. The insomnia rears its ugly head in the Williamstown dorm. (On the worst night, after reading Edith Wharton, I cry to Grandma Ida, "I'm old and alone and poor and I'm going to die like Lily Bart!" Ida replies, "You're not old.") But also that spring and summer, there are beautiful art exhibits at every museum and new friends and unsuccessful crushes. I'm too raw for casual hookups but too busy for a real relationship, and this is a terrible combination for romantic adventure. I get around anyhow: an Irish playwright, an American lighting designer, actors who are both too young and too stoned to be real matches (but maybe that's the point?), a museum guy, a film guy (he has brilliant tattoos; Chernus is appalled), and so forth. One twenty-something says, "I can't have sex with you because you're the kind of girl I want to take to museums." To which I say, "Guess what? When you grow up, you can do both with the same person."

In the fall, I start rehearsals for *Smashing* and throw myself into work. Work does not disappoint. I like to tell my students, "When you write a play, you create the world anew. You dictate its rules and its rhythms. You are not beholden to anyone else's idea of 'reality.'" And when it rehearses (in September 2003) and premieres (in October 2003, directed by the brilliant Trip Cullman and produced by The Play Company), *Smashing* is everything I love most. Noah, who it seems is reading my reviews online from the macrobiotic wife-swapping commune, calls. "Are you through trying to prove to the world that you're special?" he asks. (I think the rest of that sentence went "and ready to have babies with me?" but I'm not entirely sure because the whole thing was so insulting.)

Apparently I'm not ready for either. That fall, I leave my small "boutique" theater agents for a larger and more powerful agency that can represent me in film and television as well as stage. When I sign, the new agent says, "I'm your partner. We're going to make money." And I am relieved. I can't live in the East Village with a twenty-something actor forever. I am starting to need things I never needed before—or at least didn't recognize that I needed—a larger room, clothes that don't come from a thrift shop, health insurance. And refuge from fact-checking. That afternoon, I leave the agency, now "my" agency, and I call to tell Marilyn about this wave of good fortune. Marilyn, however, has other plans for the conversation, which she begins with: "Well, the paramedics were here today, and I almost died. What's your news?"

I get off the phone quickly and ride the F train home feeling lonely again and very, very cold.

I spend Thanksgiving making out with a stranger I've met at St. Dymphna's, and Christmas at home alone, with a cold no less, reading *The Corrections*. Despite my recent success, I'm running out of money again, so the first week in January, I go back to Condé Nast for another *House & Garden* sojourn and amp up my teaching activities. Soon I take a job as a guest artist at George Washington High School in Washington Heights—at the opposite end of Manhattan from where I currently live. The commute seems endless and involves waking up earlier than someone with my theatergoing nightlife should (it also involves more than one subway train). I try to arrive early and score cheap café con leche at the diner on the corner before classes. My favorite student, a smart-talking Lothario poet with one arm—the other lost to a birth defect—writes a poem that links blackness to invisibility. "Have you read *Invisible Man*?" I ask. But he has not. The next week, I give him my copy, saying, "I think you might like this."

One day, as an experiment, I ride the M3 bus home to see how long it takes door to door. The bus originates on upper Broadway, near the high school on Audubon Avenue, and ends in front of Cooper Union, the East Village art school a few blocks from our apartment. The ride lasts well over an hour and a half as it winds through Central Park and down Fifth Avenue. By the time I get to my neighborhood, I'm hot and sticky and need a margarita (easily obtained). And from then on, I'm resigned to the subway.

In addition to my twice-a-week stint in Washington Heights, I teach creative writing workshops in the classroom at New Dramatists on weeknights and, on Saturdays, weekend immersion classes for Discovery, a new charter high school in the South Bronx. (That commute takes even longer than the one to Washington Heights!) I have roughly four jobs at any one time, and I'm exhausted. This is when I start eating meat.

I've been sushi-vegan (total hypocrite: no eggs, meat, or

dairy, but lots of fish and ice cream) since meeting Noah in 1994—and except for the occasional burger that we'd split under dire circumstances, I have kept to the rules. But I'm cold and depressed and sad all winter—*depleted*, I think, as I find myself lying on the kitchen floor, wondering how I'll get through this strange, sad period. Finally, I go to a clinic in Chelsea for a blood test, which reveals mild iron-deficient anemia. The doctor says I can take iron pills or else "have a burger a couple times a month." Thus, I reintroduce red meat into my diet. Emma always said I should. She invented the term "vege-primacist" to explain a diet that could be primarily vegetarian but include meat for nutritional or aesthetic reasons, and she's right. After a week of lentils and brown rice, a burger and glass of red wine give me the strength to meet the outside world, to feel supported. And I need whatever help I can get right now.

Help is on its way in the form of the A-list movie star ingenue who has seen *Smashing* onstage and now decides she wants to produce and star in a movie adaptation. We meet at my favorite café to discuss the details. The starlet describes our endeavor as a grassroots backyard art project. "I'll protect you," she says, when I express concern over the massive Hollywood machinery that could get involved and potentially replace me as the writer. But she repeats, "I'll protect you." She asks how long it will take me to write a screenplay, and I promise, "If you pay me enough to quit my four teaching jobs, I can give you a first draft in a month." And I do just that. I quit all of my jobs (except for MCC) and write a screenplay in a month, living on bagels, coffee, and my Visa card until the money comes through.

Meanwhile, rehearsals are starting for my play *The Triple*

Happiness at the Second Stage Theatre, starring one of my
adolescent idols, Ally Sheedy. "Remember," I warn myself,
"not to do your high school parking lot imitation of Ally
directly to her face." Because one of the major entertain-
ments in Northbrook, Illinois, in 1987 was to recite lines
from *St. Elmo's Fire* or *The Breakfast Club* in the parking lot outside of Poppin' Fresh Pies. (No wonder I couldn't wait to
get to New York.) Simultaneously, a workshop production
of *Sam and Lucy* is in rehearsal for the Summer Play Festival.
I go back and forth between rehearsal processes working
on both plays at once. And again, I am happiest this way,
working. Two plays at the same time and a screenplay deadline? Bring it.

But as the Buddhists say, change is the only constant.
Things are tense at home. Rehearsals have me less consid-
erate and less tolerant, craving privacy. I've outgrown the
postage-stamp-size room and also the joys of a roommate.
Any roommate. When I'm annoyed with Chernus ("Do
you ever clean the bathroom?"), I can't find the justifica-
tion for "getting over it." And when he's annoyed at me,
("I'm not your boyfriend. And you owe me cab fare from,
like, eighty cab rides last month.") it stings. It is time for
my own place. I'm thirty-five years old. I want autonomy
and real furniture. I want more than one room in which
to throw dinner parties, write plays, bring guys home, and
walk around naked. (Not that I ever really walk around
naked. Really, I just want to keep writing.) I want an adult
home. And with the sale of *Smashing,* I can afford one. We
decide to give up our lease.

When I start looking for studios in the neighborhood,
I'm shocked to discover how much apartments cost in 2004.
Even *with* the movie star money, it's going to be hard. I've

been paying $800 a month to live with Chernus—the most I've ever paid to live anywhere—and still it's been a stretch to make rent each month. Studios in lower Manhattan start at $1,150, more commonly $1,200. Even better, if you want amenities like closets and bathtubs, $1,400. And although I do have this windfall right now, I can't promise that it will continue to flow—or fall—consistently. The thing about a life in the arts is that the pay scale is not consistent and growth happens intermittently—with extreme highs and lows on both counts. Totally unlike a corporate structure, in which one can see linear progression, self-employed artists can have a good year and then a bad year and then two terrible years and then a windfall—and then, who knows?

Kyra, who's recently leased her own place, talks me into more abundant thinking. "This is what apartments cost," she says, "and you have enough for first and last month's rent. You're going to take a deep breath and get an apartment and then you're going to have enough faith that you can make rent each month. That's how you do it. A deep breath—and a leap of faith."

So I'm looking. East Ninth Street, a basement that is nonetheless out of my price range. Stanton Street, a mouse problem. East Thirteenth Street, overpriced and no bathtub. State Street in Brooklyn is a possibility—there's a beautiful garden just outside the main window—but still no bathtub. On Orchard Street, I covet two studios in the same walk-up building—a bathtub, exposed brick, a sushi place downstairs—but I can't make any headway with the Israeli landlord who insists I have a guarantor or else supply something absurd, like eight months of rent in advance. I assemble a package, much like the one that Kyra and I put together six years earlier, but this time my package includes a letter from my agent, promising that my income will triple within the next year, and copies of my tax returns from the years I had playwriting awards. (The landlord is unmoved; he just wants his cash.) And then one day, stalking Craigslist, which has replaced the *Village Voice* as my favorite apartment-seeking medium, I find an ad for a 1BR on my second favorite block of the city—Mott between Houston and Prince.

Years ago, when I lived on Thompson, I used to walk across Prince Street to Bella's, a diner with mediocre food but impressive checkerboard floors and cheap breakfast specials. At that point, the neighborhood was comprised solely of Italian grandparents, Jim Jarmusch, and a dancer or two. Ten years later, it's hot real estate. Fashionistas and rock stars have joined the Italian grandparents, who are still here. Moby joins Jarmusch. On a rainy Thursday, I look at 285 Mott Street. It is perfect. I want it. I fax my application over—from my agent's office—that afternoon. The management company says they'll take the weekend to review it. The opposite of patient, as if waiting for an acceptance to college or the second phone call after a very good date, I wait.

While waiting, I spend the weekend "stalking the apartment," watching it from across the street (or from nearby Ciao Bella, where the key lime ice cream with graham cracker crust might have actual magical powers, even if I do not). I imagine funneling my energy into the building, attaching to its frequency, aligning energies, so that the landlord will somehow feel, intuitively, that I belong in his property and want me there. He'll ignore the words "self-employed" on my tax returns and focus instead on the subtle way in which I already belong. I watch my future neighbors come and go, wondering, Will I like them? Will they like me? Can this be home?

And it works! On Monday morning I get a message that my application has been accepted. I can sign my lease and move in October 1. I'm elated. The rent is $1,325 a month, which sounds ridiculous and enormous and terrifying, but like Kyra said, I'm just going to have to take a leap of faith.

....

285 Mott Street

I wake up on October 2 in my bedroom at 285 Mott Street, deliriously happy. It is one of the best days of my whole entire life. I get out of bed, feet touching the smooth wood floors—my smooth wood floors—and walk into the kitchen, admiring the light which already fills my living space and the flowers (sent by my mother) on the kitchen table. *How have I never had this before?* But I have not. Never before have I experienced complete sovereignty over my physical space, over where I live and how. It's the best feeling ever, even better than falling in love. Dizzying. Satisfying. Abundant. I think, *This apartment is a miracle. A new bottom line. Something to defend and hold on to.*

I make a pot of coffee and look around at the unpacked boxes covering every inch of floor space. They look like Christmas (or Hanukkah) presents waiting to be unwrapped. I start unpacking immediately. Again, happy beyond belief. I make a list of things I need: a lamp for the bedroom (which I realized at sunset the night before had no actual light fixture), more bookshelves, a coat rack. (There are

no closets whatsoever in the entire apartment, an inconve-
nient quirk that I will find more charming than trouble-
some.) *Thank you,* I think. *Thank you, thank you, thank you.*

Later that day, Penney comes over to bless the space and
clear its energy. I light a candle. We walk around the neighborhood. What will happen here? I wonder. Who will I be
in this space? What will unfold? Who will I love? And what
will I write?

I'm on deadline with the *Smashing* screenplay as well as
a new play commission from Arielle Tepper, producer
of the Summer Play Festival where *Sam and Lucy* debuted.
I'm used to writing in coffee shops, mostly to get away
from roommates, but Penney says this time, here, I'm
going to work at home. And work I do. I have two writing stations—one at the kitchen table and another in the
bedroom. I transit between the two while working on both
projects.

And I stay home! In fact, for weeks after moving in, all
I want to do is be inside the place, soaking it up, bonding the way a mother bonds with a newborn by placing the
baby against her body. I feel that way about my apartment.
Which means I lie around in my writing clothes (a hybrid
of pajamas and workout gear and headbands). I buy dishes
and groceries. I have people over to tea. I buy a teapot. I
start coming home at the end of my workday, eating dinner at the aforementioned tiny white retro kitchen table (a
find! Waldorf Hysteria on Avenue B!). When friends come
over, we sit on the steamer trunk that I've had since 1992,
when I made out with some guy who had the same birthday
as me (he gave me his trunk, if not his love), loaded up with
pillows and set at the table as if it were a picnic bench. And

I start to cook—more than in any previous place with the lone exception of the Princess Apartment, where Emma and I had space, light, and love for the culinary arts.

Many things happen during the three years I live here. Writing is abundant. Love is strange. Growth is undeniable. My neighbor Nancy is an angel. A seventy-something Italian former singer and tarot card reader who now works as an extra in television and harbors a secret crush on Jimmy Smits, Nancy has lived in this building *for-evah*. She offers friendship and neighborly advice, mostly on love, which she assures me is coming as soon as I stop looking and "let go." I have other friends scattered around the neighborhood—Will on Spring Street, Kyra on Prince—and colleagues. And so it always feels like a neighborhood. My neighborhood. And the first year passes.

But when *Smashing* the movie doesn't get made (some combination of flaky leadership and a fickle chain of command), I'm left scrambling to make ends meet. By the fall of 2005, I have five teaching jobs, none of which pay very well, and a ghostwriting rewrite gig on a Korean movie. I'm barely earning enough for rent and food. Desperate for cash—again—I sell off my Nanette Lepore cocktail dresses at the resale store (okay, so I bought them secondhand) and start looking for new ways of earning money. I still have the big-deal Hollywood agents. And producers come to me, wanting me to develop projects with them—for free. But I can't afford to work—pitch, outline, write, any of it— for free. I ask my agents, Is there any way, any at all, to ask for any amount of money? They say no. It's not how this part is done. I balk at being called a "baby writer" since I've been writing professionally since 1993 and working as a playwright since graduating from Juilliard in 1999. Still, with no screenwriting credits and very little understanding of the way screenwriters "pitch" their stories before writing them, I am indeed a "baby."

When *Smashing* was first optioned in 2004, crazy promises were made—the stuff of dreams, of my dreams! Impressive industry names were thrown around—directors, actors, even Madonna—as if commonplace and accessible. Agents used the first names of these megastars the way I refer to my circle of friends, assuring me that "Meryl" or "Rob" or "Jodi" would be "so into it." Managers and producers stalked me, calling more often than my mother (a feat!), trying to get a piece of what looked to them like a hot property. I was naive and hopeful enough to believe all of it. I thought that my little movie would not only get made, but made with integrity and style, in a way that respected both creative and fiscal interests. Ha! I thought—insanely and inaccurately—that my experience would prove all the stereotypes and Hollywood screenwriting war stories wrong. After all, the starlet came to me—I didn't pursue her. She "loved" the play, was "passionate about" making the movie, and had verbally promised to "protect" it. But she moved on with little to no communication, except through the producer who could offer nothing concrete or specific. I was left feeling like a Macy Gray song: "We had such a good time, Hey! Why didn't you call me?" Soon after our last communication (when she was still invested and attached), she changed her phone number and e-mail address. The door opened, and then it was abruptly and finally closed. My agents urged me to get the rights back, falsely promising that they could set the movie up without the starlet. They were wrong. When *Smashing* came back to me in 2006, my agent said that because the script had been sent out by her West Coast colleague as a writing sample, it was "over-exposed" and she couldn't set it up from New York. Which means, the gamble of leasing this apartment and increasing my overhead, has not paid off.

I try to have faith and trust creation, believing that writing will, as it has before, work everything out. In 2005 and 2006, I write three new full-length plays and two screenplays. The plays are *Hunting and Gathering* (which starts with the list of the apartments I've lived in), *A Perfect Couple* (the Tepper commission), and *Out of the Water* (a small, triangulated chamber piece set in my apartment in Nolita), but I have little planned in the way of production or commission. And every month, through the same combination of spit and chewing gum (or hard work and prayer), I am able to pay my rent. The apartment still feels like the most important thing. When friends suggest I give it up, look for something cheaper, I will not hear of it. This is my home; I have worked long and hard in order to have this home; I'm staying.

But the apartment isn't perfect. For one thing, Mott Street is like a nexus of loud people. During the day, they sit on the bench below my kitchen window eating ice cream—loudly—and talking on their cell phones—also loudly. At night, they're drunk and stumbling home from nearby hot spots or, worse yet, getting into their cars in the parking garage directly across the street from my bedroom, yelling something to their equally drunk friends that I'm sure sounds far more witty to them than it does to sleep-deprived me. Now that I actually *can* sleep, I want to! I also want to give these people a lesson in "public versus private" behavior. Then there are the quirks of the (very old) building itself. On the day that Uranus conjuncts

Pisces (electricity meeting ocean) I notice water dripping through a light fixture in my bathroom. I leave message after message for the super—a surly but ultimately kind Polish immigrant with a hat business around the corner; he is determined to dislike me, but in the end I win him over—who has to turn off my electricity entirely so as not to create a fire hazard. It takes days for him to persuade the girl upstairs to allow him access to her apartment, where he will find her air conditioner leaking water onto her floor and into my light fixture. (Who denies their super access when there's a problem affecting fire conditions in the building?)

Then the bedbugs. In July 2006, as I'm flirting with the possibility of moving to Los Angeles to jump-start my movie career, I start to itch and then notice little bug bites along my collarbone. At first I think it's mosquitoes. But they don't look like mosquito bites. A day later, I think it's poison ivy (which I'd gotten the summer before at a friend's outdoor wedding), but the bites continue and Penney says, wisely, "It's coming from your bed." Bedbugs have been an urban myth in New York City for the past year. For those of us who thrift-shop like it is a religious rite, it is a myth we both live in terror of and alternately (if the jacket is cool enough) ignore. But lately I've been hearing the stories again, and when I look online that Fourth of July weekend, after all the itching, I learn that it's an "epidemic" in both New York and London, traveling primarily through luggage and luxury hotels. And when I tear my mattress apart, looking for signs, I find one lone bug, its tiny body engorged from (my) blood. I stick the bug to a sticky trap (reserved for my fear of mice) and hand it

over to Melissa, the hip chick exterminator whom Penney
has recommended. Melissa (for a hefty fee) makes the bugs
go away while I vacate for a weeklong residency at a theater
upstate. I'm being eaten alive in the apartment that I've
been killing myself to pay for. So when Patricia, a psychic
that a playwright friend refers me to, says, "California is a
better place for you," I'm listening.

The thing is, though, Mott Street still feels like home.
I love it here. I love the colors. I love the shops—which I
can't afford to shop in but use as visual art fodder anyhow. I love the food. I love Nancy and all of my neighbors and the super who's stopped frowning every time
he sees me and the photographer next door with the "99
Luftballons" fetish and the sushi joint downstairs, where
the sushi chef has recently started slipping me freebies as
a reward for frequent patronage. I love the proximity to
nearly everything, which means I can get away with barely
ever riding the subway, taking the time to walk instead. I
love the light in my apartment in the afternoons and long
walks up and down Mott, Mulberry, and Elizabeth once
the sun has set. How could I even think of leaving? But
leave I do. Besides, lately I find myself combing the island
of Manhattan in search of an extra avenue, some corner
I have not yet seen or been kissed on. (Freeman Alley—a
tiny offshoot of Rivington Street, more like a big drive-
way than an actual street—is a revelation. Who knew that
existed?)

In the fall of 2006, I swap apartments with a playwright
from L.A.—he lives in my place and I in his—for two
months. And mostly, it's good, shooting new life into my
writing career—both plays and movies. I start dating Noah

again, who is now financially solvent and living in Pasadena. I see old friends from Chicago and Providence who have found the West to be a gracious home. I even see Wes, who has relocated and begun a second career as a yoga teacher. When the two months end and I come back to Mott Street, I'm torn. On the one hand I love L.A.—like a Wang Chung song and with a passion atypical to most New Yorkers—but I'm determined to hold on to Mott Street and my New York life, which I do for the next nine months, until the landlords raise the rent to $1,550 a month, which is way outside my means. Not only is my apartment *not* rent controlled, but in fact I signed a piece of paper when I moved in granting the landlords the right to raise the rent however and whenever they choose, according to market value. But $1,550? Really? Again I go Buddhist: "impersonal passing phenomenon . . . nothing can be held on to." In my case, certainly not a lease. I think, *Don't look for your stability in the world. Because stability isn't in the world.* I consider going back to L.A.—for good—but my play *Hunting and Gathering* is due to go into production in New York, at Primary Stages Theater, starting rehearsals on December 18. And my mom is in the hospital, again, in Detroit.

Marilyn's health has been in rocket decline since the amputation, but now it's even more dramatic. Since the start of 2007, she has been more in than out of the hospital—and I've been praying for her to be released from suffering almost daily. That July—the same week I get the news about my newly raised rent—she calls, urging me to come see her at once. When she calls, I'm in residence at the Cape Cod Theatre Project, workshopping *Out of the Water*. She acts as though I'm on vacation and not on a job, suggesting that it's selfish for me to be on Cape Cod at all when she's suffering. I do my best to explain that we're rehearsing a play, that I'm being paid to be in residence working on, editing, and rewriting the play, and far from being on vacation, I'm staying in a dorm room that smells like adolescent boys and has a mild ant infestation.

"But I'm sick," she says.

I do not say, "But you're always sick!" Instead, I repeat, as patiently as I can, "I'm on a job. And when this job ends, I have a week to go back to New York and deal with my apartment, and then two weeks in England on another job. I don't get paid if I don't show up. But more importantly"— and now I'm on a roll—"these companies have gathered resources—financing, actors, designers even—I can't just not show up! People are expecting me to do my job! And it's time-sensitive. It's not like they can postpone an entire festival, or do the play some time in the future."

She doesn't understand.

"I promise to come in August," I say, thinking that once my jobs are over and my apartment-related decisions worked through, it could be really nice to see my mom.

"If I'm alive that long!" she threatens.

"That's a really shitty thing to say," I tell her. "You're basically threatening me with your life."

I hang up on her.

A week later, the one week between Cape Cod and England, she overdoses on an over-the-counter medication and lands back in the ICU (which no longer sounds like DKNY, but now just sounds like hell) with some kind of blood clot in her lung that leads to a cardiac arrest. I put everything on hold to travel to Detroit to, once again, "say good-bye," wondering how long the torture of my mom's extended stay on death's doorstep can last. Every time I say good-bye to her, it's like reliving my worst childhood fear—the one where, after my dad dies, Marilyn dies, too, and there is no one left to love me. Every time she gets this close, the terror and grief start to replay, like a record with a skip, all over again.

I call Noah for support. But he's in a new relationship and can't talk to me. "Tell your girlfriend that my mother's dying, and you and I are friends," I tell him. But he still can't—or won't—talk. I call a few friends, and only the ones who have already lost their mothers, and there are a few, can really understand. They rally around me, offering support and kindness.

Fighting to hold on to anything at this point is too much, especially when Marilyn is released from the hospital and sent home but calls less than a week later to say, "I overdosed again. Whatever happens, I want you to know how much I loved you."

"What do you mean, you overdosed? Are you trying to commit suicide?" I ask.

"I'm trying to commit anything!" she counters.

"I don't know what that means. You don't sound like a dying person," I say.

"I just want you to know—" she repeats.

"Yes, Mother, I know. You love me. Your love is not in question. Do you need me to call 911?"

She says no, the paramedics are already on the way. ("Grandma already did that"—then, joking, "They certainly know the address.") And now, I lose it. "What am I supposed to do when you 'overdose,' and I'm in Brooklyn, New York, looking at apartment shares because I'm being priced out of my home? Is there something practical that

I can do to help you in this moment? Do you want me to drop everything, including finding a place to live, to fly in and sit by your bedside?" I demand, summoning the "tough love" tactics I learned when I was in high school and she was having those car accidents and lying in bed in the dark. Furious, she hangs up on me.

Needless to say, I'm not at my best when I let go of Mott Street and move into a share in Prospect Heights, Brooklyn—an area I've always liked for its tree-lined streets and old brownstones. The day I move into the share, I know I've made a grave mistake. As a self-employed person, with a play about to go into production and a dying parent about to go into her own production, this might not be the best time to live with a stranger. My former roommate might agree.

Marilyn spends the fall season back at Beaumont, the same hospital in which my father died twenty-nine years earlier. The nurses range from kind to severe. ("Your mother can't live here, you know," says one humorless blond hospital administrator—on my mother's sixty-fifth birthday, no less.) The care ranges from attentive (that one nurse we all liked) to unconcerned (that blonde we didn't) to downright negligent (calls from Marilyn, "They're leaving me sitting in my own shit all day"). I visit when I can, after unpacking in the new share, the weekend of her birthday, and again two weeks later, on a business trip with my temporary job, writing Webisodes for an automotive company. (The producer says, "We're having a crucial emergency team meeting tomorrow. Is there any way you could join us in Detroit?" and I say, "Gladly. So long as I can spend the night and see my mom and grandma.") It is good to see Marilyn. I touch her face and hair. I hold her hand. And I cry for days when I leave.

After just six weeks, I move out of the Brooklyn share and put my things back into Chelsea Mini-Storage. I live out of a suitcase. Everything feels strange. I take off for my first vacation in six years—two weeks in a friend's grandmother's château in the French countryside—and strangely decide to spend the next few months living much as I had in 1993 and 2002, except this time, without fear or resistance. It is a bizarre plan, one that reeks of regression and potentially nihilism. But Penney approves. And I tell myself that once the rehearsal process is over, I'll go back to L.A. I even make plans to live with a friend for the first year. So, when I return from France, I move into New Dramatists, workshopping yet another new play (*The Jesus Year*) and floating until *Hunting and Gathering* starts rehearsal on December 18. On December 16, I move my things to an apartment on Spring Street, since New Dramatists will be closed for the Christmas holidays, and Caleb, a new friend, the producer of a short film I've just written, will be out of town. His apartment, a 1BR in my old neighborhood, is small but charming, with wooden beam ceilings, scratchy rugs from Chinatown, and a Votivo red currant candle. I am so relieved to be back! I start all my old routines again—8 A.M. yoga on Houston, followed by coffee from Cafe Gitane and afternoons loitering in the bookstore on Prince Street. And then, the inevitable.

On December 17, I get a call from my grandmother saying that my mom has gone into cardiac arrest again in the hallway outside of the emergency room at Beaumont (the details are too horrible to even write about).

"What does that mean?" I ask, trying to get information before the panic sets in. She says they don't know yet. But she'll keep me in the loop. And then she shuts off her phone and goes back to the doctors. It's like being hit in the stomach, all of the air goes away. I'm standing on Fifth Avenue when I get this call. I do not know what to do, how I feel, or where to go next. I just stand in the middle of the sidewalk immobilized and freezing. Everything everywhere is cold. I have to pick a bag of my stuff up from New Dramatists (having mostly moved out of the room the day before), so I head over there but leave as soon as I remember the annual holiday party. I'm certainly not up for a party. My friend Susan meets me for overpriced lasagna across the street from Caleb's, where I'm staying, and I barely make it through that. I'm not crying, I'm not emotional, I'm just in a daze. Later that night, alone at Caleb's, I wrap myself in his blankets and wait. After so many years, so much back and forth, so many of my mother's miraculous recoveries, is this it?

The next morning I wake up (no word yet from Ida) and go to the first day of rehearsal for *Hunting and Gathering,* my play about couch-surfing and subletting. This day has been on my calendar for almost a year. Needless to say, I never imagined it would be like this. In an attempt to keep the news about my mom from the actors and designers, who are all gathered for an auspicious first day, I stay collected and brisk. Meanwhile, I spend each coffee break on the phone, desperately checking messages from my grandmother, to see if my mom is still alive. By the time the artistic director has finished his opening speech, the designers have each presented their work, and the actors have read through the play once aloud, my mom has been moved to the hospice floor of Beaumont and given enough morphine to help her die.

Leigh, the director, lets the actors go early, without saying anything about my mother but instead that she and I "need to meet." She takes me to Café Un Deux Trois, a place my mother loved, because I want to eat roast chicken, and I don't want to be alone. I'm grateful for Leigh—her ability to make a decision, her calm concern, her willingness to be with me now. I feel sad. But more than the emotion, I'm aware of the chill, the quiet, the vulnerability more than actual grief. Or, I think, maybe this is grief. Maybe this is what grief feels like. I try to eat. I try to drink. Both are hard. When it's time for Leigh to go, I call one of my closest friends, the irrepressible and sparkling Jess, who says, "Whatever you need," only I can't figure out what that is. Here is this event that I've been afraid of—and preparing for—since I was a little girl, and it's finally happening and I have no idea how to be inside of it.

I go back to Caleb's and book a ticket to Detroit. ("But I remember there being a bereavement fare that was not in fact *more than* the price of a discount ticket on Priceline," I complain to the unfeeling "service associate.") I still feel overwhelmingly cold. And there are practical, as well as emotional, reasons for that as Caleb's place doesn't have great heat, and the space heater has a tendency to blow out the electricity when anything else is turned on (stereo, toaster, you name it). I don't want to sit at home crying and feeling cold and alone. That's not what any of this is about. I want to be out in the world, the way my mother liked to be out in the world, celebrating her spirit, remembering her joy. After all, she's not dead yet—Marilyn is still

with us, and I think she wants to go out in style. Jess and I
head to Schiller's for blood orange mimosas and whatever
else feels good as we celebrate my mother. We're joined by
good friends. (And while we're waiting for a table, some
Wall Street–type dude even asks for my phone number. I
think, Marilyn's strange sense of humor from the Beyond.)
And we toast Marilyn. We drink and talk about her—her
beauty, her sense of humor, her bad choices in love, her
great choices in designer footwear, her outrageous sense of
fun. The numbness is starting to melt, replaced by a deep,
deep sadness. Most of my life I have been separating from
my mom, putting healthy distance and loving boundaries
between the often-amorphous and hard-to-define "me"
and "her"—looking for a new relationship with her, one
in which I could be fully myself, create, hold a job, earn
money, a relationship in which each of us could feel more
secure in our own, separate skins. And now, she's gone.
No more "you and me against the world," even though that
ceased to be a mantra (at least for me) years ago. When
Schiller's closes, I get into a cab and go home to Caleb's,
tearful and dreading the call, which comes a few hours later,
at 4:30 A.M., telling me that my mom is gone. Ida and I cry
together a little, but mostly we are relieved that Marilyn is
no longer suffering, that she's free. It's been such a long,
long journey—in many ways hardest for Ida, who says, "A
parent shouldn't have to bury a child."

I'm on a plane five hours later. I ask Noah to come to
the funeral with me—he had once promised he would—
but now he says in a voice mail message, "I understand
that this is a big deal for you...but it would make
things uncomfortable at home, for me." We do not speak
again.

Marilyn's funeral is quiet. I think I won't be able to stand seeing her laid out in the coffin (terrible memories of my father just so), but she looks peaceful and pretty, finally at rest. She is buried with one of her hand-stitched "Marilyn" handkerchiefs and a whole lot of roses. My grandmother wanted pink, but I remember my mom telling me a joke between her and my dad from the night of their first date. After he joked to her that if she didn't go out with him and instead stayed home to eat a tuna sandwich, as she'd said she wanted to, she would die of botulism, Marilyn had told Harvey, "Well, if I do, you can bring yellow roses to my funeral. Because that's what I like." He brought them to their first date, a week later. And she brought them to his funeral some fifteen, sixteen years after that. I make sure there are some at hers.

I spend a few more days with my grandmother. I start looking through my mom's drawers and files, reading her journals and then old letters to her, from me. I even sleep in her bed, wrapping myself in her enormous down comforter, which does, in fact, keep me warm. Then, after the Christmas holidays, I head back to New York City and rehearsal. The actors now know about my mother and have been working on the play without me, writing down their questions, keeping track of lines they want me to look at or adjust. As usual, work offers solace. And for the next six weeks, I accept that solace, throwing myself into the production. And it's great, although I joke with my therapist that mascara is something I should abstain from entirely. Every time I put it on in the morning, I think, There's no way I'll cry today. And then, of course, I cry—black rivers down my face, residue, raccoon eyes, circles—I look battered. I'm sure I'm doing damage to my skin just wiping the mascara stains away. My mother would probably tell me not to wipe my eyes like that for fear of causing wrinkles. And hearing her admonish me, in my head, only makes me cry more.

The morning after opening night, I go back to Detroit, where I clean out Marilyn's enormous storage space. Not only does she have a small "locker" like everyone else in the building, but somehow my mom persuaded the management to let her take over the power-supply room on her floor—where she stored everything else. And I mean *everything*. Marilyn kept *everything*. After years of letting go of excess, becoming "light," I spend these weeks throwing away everything from my baby teeth (wrapped in paper towel and stored in a Tiffany's box) to photographs of The Archduke and his second wife (Why did Marilyn even *have* these pictures?), sorting through everything with the somber knowledge that I can't keep any of it. My mom and I had always assumed that someday I'd have a "basement"—a place to store things—as she had (or at least a power-supply room). My mom and I also talked about her basement (and later her storage space) as a place where I could keep things indefinitely. No more. And while my life had been predominantly about shedding, hers was about holding on. And now that hers was over, I am left holding boxes full of stuff: my school report cards, my Girl Scout uniform, anytime I ever put a crayon to a page—plus letters from my father's divorce lawyer and photographs and keepsakes and record albums of her life with him and then with me. I throw away and donate anything that I can't keep, thinking that it's a ritual to help free my mother's soul and lighten her load. In death if not in life. And strangely, I'm the only person who has the ability to do this very thing. It may be my superhero power—letting go.

It's almost time to settle down again. But first I have to go back to New York and close the play. I move back into New Dramatists for a few weeks, and then, when the Composer-Librettist Studio needs the dorm rooms, into my friend Trip's beautiful guest room (affording me the opportunity for wonderful dinners with Trip, "food porn" cooking shows, and my first taste of Wii). Something is new, though. I am strangely at peace. It's *fine* to be on the go like this, living out of two suitcases (and a third for a few of my mom's things, which I'm carrying with me). And I do like the company. And it's clear to me that most of this last year I've been waiting for Marilyn, who I have known was close to death since those hospital stays in April 2007, if not before. ("They're trying to kill me with insulin. And if they kill me, I need you to know I wrote everything down. For you.") Now that she's gone, I'm free to go wherever I want.

I am also free in another way. For many years, I'd been aware of a desire to keep good things, fortune, hidden away. This irrational and often nonverbal fear stated that if I experienced fortune, my mother would either (1) be jealous and claim it as hers or (2) die. Now that she's gone, there is nothing more to hide. There is no one to appease or bargain with. There is no one to be afraid of losing. I'm free to love her without restriction. For years, I tried to maintain iron-clad boundaries, often keeping my mom at arm's length in order to do very basic things— pursue work, show up on time, spend a day at a temp job without any hysterical personal calls, pay my bills, sleep through the night. We talked (and yelled and cried and proclaimed our love) at every single juncture, every single time, as battle lines were drawn and later redrawn. But the choices themselves were hard, and they weighed on us both. The boundaries were hard. And our relationship was hard. And now, those boundaries melt away. I can let my mother into my heart fully and entirely. We're no longer fighting and so I can fully receive her beautiful and stubborn heart.

I briefly try to get a new apartment in lower Manhattan, but after a series of dreams about canyons and "Mariposa Street" I decide to give L.A. another shot. I line up a place there, a share in my friend Rick's downtown loft. Just as this plan is coming together, I receive two opportunities. The first is a residency at the MacDowell Colony, a haven for artists, writers, filmmakers, musicians, and digital and performance artists in the woods of New Hampshire. The second opportunity, set for my return from the woods, will be an Off-Broadway production of my play *A Perfect Couple* with Sasha Eden and Victoria Pettibone, two stellar women with a production company called WET. I say yes to both. I tell Rick not to expect me until July and then I find what I believe to be my last temporary sublet—for the post-MacDowell/pre—new life in L.A. rehearsal period. After *Hunting and Gathering* closes, I take one more trip to visit Grandma Ida, then get on a bus from New York heading north for Peterborough and respite.

At MacDowell, artists-in-residence, called "colony fellows," are given studio space to work, a dorm room to live, and time. I have been yearning for all three. After a year of producing (and dealing), I need to rest, refuel, recalibrate, fill up again, and listen. And finally, with these three gifts— space to work, room to live, and, most precious, time—I have the space and freedom to properly mourn my mother.

On the first day at MacDowell, I am shown to my studio, where I notice the baby grand piano in the center of the

room and start to cry, thinking of my mom. I know, lament-
fully and sweetly, that Marilyn is with me. I remember a
story she used to tell about being accepted to the prestigious
music camp, Tanglewood, when she was a teenager. The
story goes, Marilyn got into Tanglewood, in faraway Massachusetts, and Ida sent her there in a car with two cute
neighborhood boys. ("She let you drive? In a car with two
boys? You'd never let me do that!" I said in protest, upon
hearing the story as a teenager.) When Marilyn and the
neighborhood boys arrived, she got out of the car, looked
around, and—terrified—declared, "I can't stay here." And
the boys drove her home (after, I think, maybe a weekend
with their families on the Cape?). So now I look around at
the artist's studio at MacDowell, the very studio in which
Thornton Wilder wrote *Our Town*, thinking, Some spell has
been broken. Some magic released. Because I'm here. And
I'm not turning around and leaving. Marilyn accomplished
what she set out to by creating a daughter who could stay.

The next seven weeks are extraordinary. Many afternoons, in between journaling and writing my screenplay, I
sit in the rocking chair next to the piano, drink hot tea, and
fondly, sadly recall, my mom. It's a nice kind of mourning, more about remembering and celebrating beauty than
about wishing she were still alive. She suffered so pro-
foundly during the last fifteen years of her life—I am happy
for her to be, as Penney assures me she is, free. I make an
altar for both my parents near the piano—Marilyn's pass-
port picture from 1973, Harvey's business card (which I've
recently found), some tree bark, a Rilke poem—and spend
time remembering and honoring them. This feels sacred.
As do the quiet walks in the snow, time alone, and every
interaction with fellow artists-in-residence.

Since Marilyn's death, I've been trying to take care of myself in a different way, mothering myself. And this new, more protective regime includes a conscious break from dating, flirting, hookups, fix-ups, and Noah (who is, after fourteen years, no longer a part of my life!). On the day of the funeral, some three months earlier, I complained to a friend, long-distance, that I had asked each of the men I'd been involved with that year to come to Detroit and be with me at the funeral. Each of them said no. "What's that about?" asked my friend. "I make bad choices in love," I quipped back. But then, more earnestly, I said, "I haven't created situations in which anyone felt a sense of responsibility or commitment. So it's not them. It's me! I need to learn to do all of this differently. . . . And until I do, I'm closed for business." Thus, I have been closed for business. And as for Noah, now I think maybe he had the clarity and vision the week my mother died to step away and let me find support from someone who could really show up. Maybe he was ready to let me go. I remember now that it felt surprisingly liberating at that funeral to acknowledge that I didn't need a man beside me. My friend Susan, who knew and loved my mom, came—flying in from Georgia, just for the day. Other friends called or e-mailed; it was enough. So no flirtations. Also, since December, I've been turning inward more and more, going inside for answers. MacDowell in winter (March is still winter in New Hampshire) is perfect for this process. The tiny stone cottage, the dorm room, the group meals. . . . it is like a cocoon, enclosed and safe. Everything I love is here: art and music and writing and occasionally a really good all-night dance party. And it is at just this moment, during the luxurious and creative process of writing and mourning and rewiring and dancing, that I meet my love.

The day after kissing Gordon, a fellow writer, I say, "You should know, I'm moving to L.A. in a few months, so . . . don't get attached."

His response: "I'd follow you anywhere."

I look at him funny, then I kiss him again. And I'm amazed at how utterly perfect and right it feels. We start spending time together, talking, driving, dancing, and telling jokes. It amazes me that I can open my heart to Gordon without feeling torn apart. I can experience him without the wave of longing and pain that I previously associated with romantic love and Eros. He is everything good. And, as my friend Rob once promised the right person would, Gordon changes my very definition of love.

Gordon goes back to the city before me. A week or two later, when my residency ends, he commands, "Come home to me." And I do. I've arranged a sublet uptown, but I don't spend more than a night there. Instead, Gordon and I borrow a friend's truck and take my things out of storage, unpacking them in his rent-controlled Dutch Kills 1BR. Dutch Kills is a tiny forgotten neighborhood around the Queensboro Bridge, on the border of Long Island City and Astoria, not far from the sublet I stayed in just after my exodus from Emma's during the spring of 2002. On uneasy nights that summer, we walk past the block I lived on, but I can't identify the building, just the feeling of despair, of being banished, and the taste of the cheap ice cream I used to buy at Food World on my walk home. How strange, I think, to be back in the neighborhood under such radically different circumstances. No despair. No banishment. No cheap ice cream. Instead, abundant kisses and moderately priced Rioja.

One night, I take him to my friend Francine's loft for dinner. She lends him a book and says, "If you guys break up, I want my book back."

"We're never breaking up," answers Gordon.

"Nice," counters Francine, impressed by his confidence and his desire for longevity.

Later, on the B61 bus heading back to Queens, I ask, "What does that mean? We're *never* breaking up?"

He says, "I am never breaking up with you. I want to be with you forever."

"Forever! I've lived in thirty apartments in twenty years and I come from divorced parents; what is this 'forever' of which you speak?"

But Gordon says "forever" and means it. And I am racing along, trying to keep up.

A day or two later, we're in his kitchen, cooking dinner and telling each other stories about our respective days (his writing, mine in rehearsal), when I realize what he's talking about.

"You mean, we get to do THIS every day?" I am incredulous.

And he says, "Yes. We get to do this. Every day."

And I start to cry. And he holds me. And we kiss again.

This is uncharted territory. An everyday love. A love that is home. I have never had this. And now I understand what it's all about. And how much I want it.

Still, I'm suspicious at first, sure that there must be some deep latent codependent flaw to the whole thing.

"He wants to see me every day," I complain on the phone to Lucy. "He wants me to come home."

"And that's a problem, why?" she asks.

"I'm not used to it. The other night, he asked if I was planning to come home for dinner, and I turned around and freaked out all over him, until I realized he just wanted to cook for me."

Giggling, Lucy says, "Honey, that's what a relationship is."

Really? It's not what any relationship I have ever been in before has remotely looked like. This is new. The love that Gordon offers is tangible and present—for everyday usage and yet holy.

I'm proud of the experiences that have led me to this moment, transience included. They have made me whole, teaching me about impermanence, faith, and creation. They toughened me up, while opening my heart. As all the healers promised, the world *did* change. (And is still changing!) And we changed, too. (And there is more ahead, I'm sure.) Everyone I know has had to open wider, let go of attachments, start to heal and transform. And through loss, we discover what we're made of, who we really are, what's essential—which is (as the Little Prince says) invisible. I wouldn't trade any of it. Transience and lack of material security were the price paid for pursuing my dream, for becoming the person I wanted to become. And now, twenty years later, I can say it has been a successful endeavor. I have the life I asked for. I'm a writer and theater artist, living in both New York City and downtown Los Angeles, earning my living through creativity. I write plays, I write movies, I write fiction and nonfiction. I teach others to do the same. Not having ever *had* financial security, or a well-heeled family nearby to rely upon, I know how to be scrappy if need be. And I have faith in the process of creation itself. I believe we are led. And that the more we let go, the easier it will be to listen, to find our way home—literally, figuratively—to our deepest dreams and truest selves.

While I can speak to faith and persistence, Gordon brings something else to the table entirely: certainty and commitment. When he says "forever," he means it. And we're about to get married, which means I will learn about "forever," too, making a commitment to him that will, I hope, last for the rest of our lives. Buddhist author Susan Piver says, in an article for *Shambhala Sun,* that when she married her husband, she "said yes to the unfolding, impenetrable arc of uncertainty. . . . I thought that finding love was an endpoint, that some kind of search was over and I would find home. . . . But really we stepped through a crazy looking glass. No matter how hard we tried, how madly in love we were, or how skillfully we planned our life together, there was complete uncertainty about what the connection would feel like from day to day. . . . I didn't really understand that love does not arise, abide, or dissolve in connection with any particular feeling. . . . Love has become a container in which we live." I can commit to that, a container within which Gordon and I will live. And receive each other. And try, day to day, to be mindful, present, and kind.

Sometimes I take him to Nolita, to the restaurants and bars I frequented when I lived on Mott Street, which I still think of as mine in some way. But everything changes. To deny change is to deny life. And the present moment contains miracles. Including an ability to see and receive the new.

There are still uncertainties, many of them. I still feel a wave of shame every time I fill out a "change of address" form with the U.S. Postal Service. And sometimes I still

reach for the phone to call my mother, forgetting momen-
tarily that she's gone. (In the grocery store, I'll hear her
voice calling me, "come, child," as when we used to move
through the aisles together, me always slightly behind her,
touching everything.) But mostly, I think, It's amazing how
I can feel her, now, with me. And I tell her, "Look how far
we can travel, Mommy. And look how good it is!" Because
it is good!

I have learned to trust the path as it unfolds.

I can say now that I have many homes. My work is home.
The family I am building with Gordon is home. A renewed
relationship with my grandmother, my community of
friends, Penney, New Dramatists, the theater, my yoga
practice . . . each of these is a component of home. The rest
keeps unfolding.

acknowledgments

First, I have to thank Julia Pastore, my editor at Random House, for asking, "Do you think there's a book in all of this?" There was! And Swanna MacNair for being my first and favorite book agent. Thanks to Jill McElroy for leading me to Swanna and cheering me on, and Rio Hernandez for leading me to Jill and for believing and pushing me.

The next round of exuberant thank-yous goes to every person I have ever lived with—you know who you are. And thank you. Especially if I forgot to clean the bathtub. You each taught me the meaning of home. And who we come home to.

An enormous thank-you to Penney Leyshon for teaching me, healing me, inspiring me, and believing in me all these many years. And for saying that someday, I'd make money.

Thank you to my grandmother, Ida Lucas, who gave me her remarkable work ethic, her love of coffee, and her Vuitton bag. Thank you for being the woman you are.

Thank you to my beautiful mother, Marilyn Berman, who is no longer with us, but who knows what's happening anyway (and, if I know her at all, is pulling a few strings). To Marilyn, I say, Look! It's all working out! A more somber thank-you to my father, Harvey Berman, who I am told wanted to be a writer himself—I hope you're taking care of my mom on the other side, and that both of you have found freedom.

Thank you to everyone at New Dramatists, most especially Todd London, Emily Morse, Joel Ruark, Ron Riley, and Jennie Greer. Thank you for an amazing seven years and for always welcoming me home.

Here, in no specific order, are a bunch of other heartfelt acknowledgments to people who loved, shared, supported, and laughed: Rick Gradone, Trip Cullman, Josh Hecht, Michael Chernus, Lucy Thurber, Leigh Silverman, Kiley Bates, Francine Volpe, Sarah Saffian, Jessica Piranian, Denyce Mylson, Michael O'Brien, Diana Gasperoni, Patricia Strasberg, The MacDowell Colony, The Corporation of Yaddo, the Eugene O'Neill Theater Center, and The Juilliard School.

And to my mentors, Marsha Norman (thank you, Marsha, for teaching me to make my plays look like plays!) and Christopher Durang, Maria Irene Fornes, Anne Bogart, and Tina Shepard.

And finally, a very special thank-you to my brilliant fiancé, Gordon Haber, who as I said in the book has changed my very definition of love. I am honored to be your wife.

Brooke Berman is an award-winning playwright whose work has been produced across the United States. She is a two-time recipient of both the Francesca Primus and Lecompte du Nouy awards; she is a recipient of a Berilla Kerr Award, a Helen Merrill Award for Emerging Playwrights, and a commissioning grant from the National Foundation for Jewish Culture for the play *Until We Find Each Other*, which was produced at Steppenwolf in 2002, directed by Anna D. Shapiro. Brooke's play *Hunting and Gathering* premiered at Primary Stages Theater, directed by Leigh Silverman, and was named one of the Ten Best of 2008 by *New York* magazine.

Brooke has taught playwriting and creative writing as a guest artist in the New York City public school system and at assorted colleges (Eugene Lang, Fordham University, University of Rochester, etc.) as well as privately through the "24 With 5 Teaching Collective," which she co-created at New Dramatists. Brooke spent four years as Director of the Playwrights Unit for MCC Theater's Youth Company, a free after-school program for NYC youth. Brooke is a graduate of The Juilliard School, and she attended Barnard College in NYC (where she was set to major in American Studies and Dance, before leaving to work with Anne Bogart). She is a member of the Dramatists Guild and an alumna of New Dramatists.

Her plays include: *Hunting and Gathering* (Primary Stages); *Smashing* (The Play Company); *Until We Find Each Other* (Steppenwolf Theatre Company); *The Triple Happiness* (Second Stage Theater); *Sam and Lucy* (SPF); *A Perfect Couple* (Arielle Tepper Productions, WET); *Out of the Water, The Jesus Year; Casual Encounters* (developed through The New Dramatists Creativity Fund), and many others. Her short play *Dancing with a Devil* was co-winner of The Heideman Award at Actors Theater of Louisville and presented as part of "Life Under 30" at the Humana Festival in 1999. The play was nominated for an American Theater Critics Best New Play award that year and was published in numerous anthologies. Her short play, *Defusion,* has been produced in assorted festivals and published in *The Backstage Book of New American Short Plays* and presented as part of Christine Jones's "Theater for One" project at New York Theatre Workshop. Brooke has twice developed work at The Eugene O'Neill Theater Center and at theaters and residencies including: the Royal Court Theatre in London, The Royal National Theatre in London, Pentabus Theatre, Soho Rep, MCC, SPF, Rattlestick, ARS Nova, Naked Angels, the Playwrights Center in Minneapolis, Childrens Theater Company in Minneapolis, The Cape Cod Theater Festival, Williamstown Theater Festival, The Hourglass Group, Primary Stages, and New Dramatists. She has been a MacDowell Colony fellow and a resident at the Corporation of Yaddo.

Brooke's short film *All Saints Day,* directed by Will Frears, won Best Narrative Short at the Savannah Film Festival and played at the Tribeca Film Festival in 2008.

www.brookeberman.net